CANCEL CULTURE

AND THE LEFT'S LONG MARCH

EDITED BY DR KEVIN DONNELLY

Turning and turning in the widening gyre
The falcon cannot hear the falconer;
Things fall apart; the centre cannot hold;
Mere anarchy is loosed upon the world,
The blood-dimmed tide is loosed, and everywhere
The ceremony of innocence is drowned;
The best lack all conviction, while the worst
Are full of passionate intensity.

The Second Coming – William Butler Yeats

ACKNOWLEDGEMENTS

The seed for this collection of essays exploring cancel culture and the origins of the culture wars was planted by the Sydney academic Catherine A. Runcie, the editor of *Reclaiming Education* and a cultural warrior in her own right.

Thanks must also be given to Kristian Jenkins, John Anderson and the Board of the Page Research Centre who all readily agreed to support this anthology from concept to publication. Without their help, advice and support the task may have proved impossible.

Those who financially supported the book's publication should also be thanked as should Michael Wilkinson and Jess Lomas from Wilkinson Publishing for their willingness to be involved in what is such an urgently needed exposé of the significance and impact of the Left's long march through the institutions.

The success of any anthology depends on the research, analysis and critique undertaken by the various authors and their ability to communicate what can often be complex and obscure. My role of editor has been made much easier as a result of those contributing exceeding what is required.

Given the dominance and pervasiveness of cancel culture and political correctness in Western societies like Australia it is crucial citizens are provided with all sides of the debate instead of being indoctrinated with cultural-left group think. If this anthology serves that purpose it has proven its worth.

Dr Kevin Donnelly

Published by:
Wilkinson Publishing Pty Ltd
ACN 006 042 173
PO Box 24135
Melbourne, Vic 3001
Ph: 03 9654 5446
www.wilkinsonpublishing.com.au

Reprinted April 2021

A catalogue record for this book is available from the National Library of Australia

Planned date of publication: April 2021
Title: Cancel Culture and the Left's Long March
ISBN(s): 9781925927566

Design by Spike Creative Pty Ltd
Ph: (03) 9427 9500
spikecreative.com.au

Printed and bound in Australia by Ligare Pty Ltd.

CONTENTS

FOREWORD

With four books on how political correctness is hurting us, and now this volume of essays against the left's long march through the institutions, Dr Kevin Donnelly AM has established himself as one of Australia's foremost culture war warriors.

This is a war that needs to be fought. If Australia is to flourish, all of us must be confident that, on balance, we can be proud of our country's history and institutions. For most of our national existence, it was all-but-taken-for-granted that we could; but not so now.

The assault on Australia Day is perhaps the most obvious example of the taint of illegitimacy now pervading our national life.

By ordaining that all subjects on the national school curriculum be taught from an indigenous, Asian and sustainability perspective, officialdom has exposed its anti-Australian prejudice. Far from being proud of a country that attracts migrants from across the globe, is amongst the freest and fairest societies on Earth, and has achieved a fine balance between humans and nature, there's a dominant left-establishment view that Australia is essentially racist, exploitative, unfair and founded on an act of fundamental injustice.

By all means, let people argue that position if they have evidence to back it up but the lived experience of the vast majority of Australians is against them. It's almost impossible to find a migrant who isn't abundantly satisfied with moving to Australia. Outside a small clique of ideological malcontents and professional activists, it's almost impossible to find a citizen who's not barracking for Team Australia.

Yet the intellectual heights are dominated by those expounding the 'negative nationhood' view. That's why books like this are important and why Kevin Donnelly has become such a key figure in our national conversation.

To me, one of the most disappointing features of our public life is the reluctance of people who know better to state what's obvious.

Business leaders should affirm the importance of free markets; union leaders should assert the basic decency of Australian workers; cultural leaders should proclaim the achievements of the Australian version of English-speaking civilisation; historians should tell the whole truth of our continent with its triumphs and joys, as well as injustices, and political leaders should be reassuring our citizens that our country is fundamentally good and getting better all the time.

Instead, business leaders are only too ready to jump on activists' bandwagons; unions campaign against their own member's jobs on environmental grounds or power-based self-interest; and supposedly conservative politicians routinely change the subject rather than discuss taboo issues like climate change, identity, gender, religious freedom and whether statues should be toppled.

Well, not before time, this book brings an antidote to the politics of division and despair.

Former prime minister Tony Abbott discerns a loss of cultural self-confidence behind our over-reaction to the pandemic. Ian Plimer debunks the claim that Australia can save the planet on its own. Anthony Dillon points out that more personal responsibility is the key to Aboriginal advancement. And there's more.

As even the honest left is starting to appreciate, we need more voices in our debates, not fewer. Wholesome diversity means a range of views, not just a multiplicity of genders and ethnicities.

As Abbott has often said, 'a majority that stays silent does not long remain a majority'. While not everyone will agree with all the viewpoints put forward here, or even most of them, no one could deny that a strong case is made by the authors.

If you want to influence our country in any direction at all, you have to speak up.

That's what all these authors have done. They've spoken up for the country, the values and the policies they believe in. Not for them—the stifling conformity with green-left orthodoxy that has so dumbed down our universities and now threatens our media and national discourse.

Kevin Donnelly has done his bit with this book. Now it's over to the rest of us to speak up if our country is to be as good as it should be. No longer can we hope 'someone else will do it' because if not us, then who?

Peta Credlin
Sky News Anchor
News Corp National Columnist
Honorary Professorial Fellow, University of Melbourne

INTRODUCTION

Imagine a society where people, from high to low, are fired from their jobs for entering into the 'wrong side' of a cultural debate, where academics are routinely sacked or sanctioned for expressing incorrect views on climate or sexuality or politics, where celebrities are stripped of accolades and authors are disinvited from award ceremonies for harbouring opinions that fail to accord with the prevailing view.

Imagine a society where students inform on their professors for transgressing speech codes, where priests are brought before tribunals for teaching the tenants of their faith, where multiple institutions from the police to the media to the courts collude to imprison an innocent man because he holds to a purer ethic they deem dangerous and obsolete. A society where people are encouraged to inform on their neighbours, where a pregnant woman is arrested in her home for posting on social media, where the police violently arrest people for breaking newly invented laws compelling them to cover their faces. Imagine a society where the citizens are arbitrarily confined to their homes by the government, their movements tracked and traced.

This isn't a passage from a mid-century dystopian novel. It's not an account of conditions suffered under totalitarian regimes in the Soviet Union, China or North Korea. No… this is contemporary Australia. All the events described have occurred in Australia in recent years, yet this is but a spattering. To list all the things in this category that have occurred around the former liberal, Western, democratic nations would doubtless require volumes.

What is going on? This anthology will go some way to answering that.

Australia, like the other Western democracies, is heir and benefactor of uniquely Western concepts like the rule of law, popular sovereignty, political and religious freedom, free and fair elections, the right to own property, the free market, the universal provision of health and education, an independent academy, a free and impartial press, human rights and Judeo-Christian ethics including the equality of all people and a commitment to the common good. These concepts have been refined and perfected down through the centuries—hard won, often through blood—and yet they are now all under serious threat.

Some may say this is fear mongering but consider the facts.

The rule of law probably won't apply if the defendant is politically suspect. After the 2016 election President Donald Trump was impeached by the US Congress on false pretences because his political opponents hate him and what he stands for. And he occupied the highest office in the land. Scant chance for you or me then. Cardinal George Pell was falsely imprisoned despite his provable innocence because he is a thorn in the side of radical secularists committed to erasing Christianity from the public square.

Political freedom wasn't available to political provocateur Milo Yiannopoulos when he was banned from entering Australia for alleged racism. Religious freedom was withheld from footballer Israel Folau who was sacked by Rugby Australia for posting a passage on social media quoting the Holy Bible. And the Australian author of *#MenToo* Bettina Arndt has been no-platformed by activist students and demands have been made to strip her of her Order of Australia simply because she defends men's rights.

The technocratic elites at the World Economic Forum show in their 2030 Agenda that they want to use the COVID-19 pandemic as a pretext to abolish property ownership (except their own, presumably). We're told that by 2030 none of us will own property or much else besides, and we're all going to be happier apparently. The document published by the World Economic Forum detailing these plans is entitled *The Great Reset*.

Education will be provided to your children, but only on the condition that you don't object to their indoctrination in radical sexual theories, climate catastrophism and the supposed evils of Western civilisation.

The academy is probably the least independent institution of all. Barely a week goes by without report of some academic somewhere losing tenure for transgressing some recently dreamt up woke doctrine, knowingly or otherwise.

An impartial press? What a joke! The majority of the mainstream media, particularly in the United States, is little more than a propaganda factory for one side of politics. Most people know it too. The media routinely ranks top of the list of the least trusted institutions, closely followed by government.

As for the Christian inspired doctrines of human rights and the equality of all people, well, they only apply to you if you're not a Christian.

The facts are plain. Nobody anymore can deny this is taking place; that this phenomenon is real and is spreading through our society and its institutions like a ravening virus.

But what is it exactly, this scourge of censorship, doctrinaire group think and political subterfuge? The pages that follow will unfold the answer with more detail and precision than can be managed here, but the title of this book is a good place to start.

Cancel Culture and the Left's Long March.

Cancel Culture refers to the process where activists drive opinion forcing institutions to 'cancel' long dead luminaries because of sins committed when they were alive that contravene contemporary woke ethics, such as failing to condemn racism back then with sufficient zeal. Or when people are set upon by online mobs for breaking woke codes, often leading to them losing their jobs, as happened to a struggling West End performer in London who was sacked from the cast of a musical because she reiterated the biblical teaching on marriage on Facebook four years previously. We could go on...

But Cancel Culture is just the latest iteration of a deeper and wider malaise that can be summarised by the other phrase in the book's title—the Left's Long March (through the institutions). We're getting closer now to the crux of the quandary. Notice that it's the left's long march through the institutions. That's right, in case you hadn't worked it out by now, all this cancelling and censoring and shaming and screeching is a tactic of the political left.

The Neo-Marxists, the Postmodernists, the Greens, socialists, lefties, call them what you will. The left's long march through the institutions is just that, a left-wing political strategy to gradually infiltrate the institutions of the West—government, the media, the Church, the family, education, culture and the arts, business, sport and so on—and to subvert them into drivers of left-wing political ideology. And in this strategy they have succeeded, which is why government policy so often leans left regardless of which party is in power; why the mainstream media is almost exclusively left-wing in its bias; why many Christian churches have sold out to the sexual revolutionaries by sanctioning same-sex marriage in direct defiance of the dictates of the ancient and venerable faith; why education, school and tertiary, is steeped in the various sub-categories of leftism; why movies, books and music bombard us with political correctness, critical theory and radical feminism; and why businesses lecture us sanctimoniously and virtue signal as Gillette did, berating their mostly male customers for their 'toxic masculinity' (and losing millions of customers into the bargain).

By why the need for all this frenzied politicking? Why does the left, broadly speaking, feel compelled to take the long march through society's institutions and use them to disseminate their ideologies and suppress opposing views? What is wrong with mainstream political and cultural opinion, why does it need subverting and cleansing? And why can't the left make its arguments openly in the public square, subjecting them to proper debate and scrutiny? Why this sneaky plot in the shadows to infiltrate institutions?

In answering such questions we ought to consider the left-wing mindset. The nativity of the modern left took place in France around the time of the French Revolution towards the end of the eighteenth century. The Jacobins and other revolutionary forces were disillusioned with the injustices of the time. An absolute monarchy colluded with rapacious nobles and a corrupt Catholic Church to concentrate power and wealth in their own hands at the expense of everybody else.

Justifiably, political groups and radicalised citizens wanted to end this by overthrowing the status quo.

What's wrong with that? Not a lot at a glance. So why did the French Revolution end in The Great Terror and the execution of tens of thousands of French citizens? It's for the same reason that the Russian Revolution led to the gulags and the Great Purge, and the Chinese Communist Revolution led to the Cultural Revolution, culminating in the deaths of millions upon millions of Russian and Chinese citizens, and legions of citizens of other countries besides.

In the end it comes down to a sense of proportion.

What we invariably discover is that the excitable young rabble rousers have gotten a little bit ahead of themselves. They fondly imagine, in their unseasoned youth, that they are the first dauntless adventurers to discover the principle of justice, and its inevitable foil, injustice. Incandescent, they set out pumped full of righteous indignation determined to overturn oppression and inequality. But in their exuberance they overlook vital facts. Yes, a fallen and imperfect world made up of fallen and imperfect people is bound to be subject to injustice in places. But the thing is, wiser heads than theirs have spotted this already and have over time written into the laws, constitutions and institutions safeguards like the separation of powers, democratic principles, the rule of law, free speech and so on, precisely to guard against the overreach of power by those that hold it.

It's inevitably more complicated than this, granted, but the conditions remain. We live in an imperfect and fallen world made up of morally compromised human beings. This has been recognised already by the elders and in their wisdom, beginning with the New Testament and a belief in the inherent dignity of the person, they have done a fair job of developing safeguards that have stood the test of time. Imperfect safeguards no doubt, but this world is imperfect.

And then along come the new kids on the block. Heads and hearts throbbing with new-fangled political zeal, their only solution to tear it all down and, in its place, build an imagined future. Such is their misplaced conviction that any opponent of this 'self-evident good' must be nothing less than mad, bad and dangerous and will have to be done away with. Killed if necessary. And here we are back where we started at the Great Terror, the Great Purge, the Cultural Revolution, all elegantly illustrated by George Orwell's metaphoric *Animal Farm*; what begins as a utopian ideal inevitably ends up enforcing even greater oppression and loss of freedom.

The ambitious young Robespierres of the world won't be hindered. History has already determined the outcome and any delay in its realisation is blamed on the forces of reaction. Therefore, they must be silenced or die … and the blood keeps flowing.

In essence this is the root cause of all the incessant leftist overreach. The radicals and the revolutionaries of the left identify genuine injustice and determine to fix it. All well and good so far, but from the outset their objectives are built on faulty foundations. Unlike liberals and conservatives—who also want to address injustice but recognise the necessity to do so gradually, sometimes, and sensitively, always, careful to keep what works and cautious of unintended consequences—leftists see injustice as evidence that the whole edifice is rotten and oppressive and must be pulled down in entirety, beams, bricks, buttresses, the lot. Out goes the bath water, along with the baby, the bath and the rubber ducky. And if pig-headed reactionaries don't get it they deserve to suffer the consequences. The Great Terror, the Great Purge, the Cultural Revolution.

So, there we have it. That's why the left MUST dominate the institutions. They are the enlightened ones who know what's best for society, and if society can't see that because it's bigoted and parochial, then the enlightened ones are left with little choice but to take over society and mould it into the utopia they must have.

Such is the rationale for the long march through the institutions, which has led us to cancel culture and the other choice delicacies of leftism. The plebs in the past, ignorant of their best interests, weren't buying the revolution. Lefty 'intellectuals' saw this and determined that the institutions of the West were to blame. The Church, the family, the media etc. were collectively responsible for brainwashing the plebs into believing that liberalism, democracy, capitalism and Christianity gave the best returns. What could be done? Well, how about we infiltrate all the institutions, gradually subvert them and eventually turn them into bastions of left-think? Then we can leverage them to re-educate everyone in the 'truth'. And that is precisely what they have done.

No area of public policy or debate is untouched. In the chapters that follow eminent experts in various disciplines—history, universities, climate science, Indigenous Australia, gender, education, the law—will show how this insidious leftist take over is now almost complete. How every area of public and increasingly private life is damaged by this corrosive ideology. Many ordinary people will be shocked to learn how far this leftist long march through our institutions has gone and what it means for us in the West. What it means for our way of life, for our families, for our children.

But let us not lose heart altogether. A fight back is taking place all across the West. The majority Brexit vote in the UK and the election of Boris Johnson's Conservative government, President Trump's election victory in 2016 and the Coalition victory in Australia in 2019 are all popular repudiations of the leftist narrative that we're all constantly force-fed. This anthology also lends its modest weight to the fight.

Onwards.

Kristian Jenkins
Executive Director, Page Research Centre

THE ORIGINS OF CANCEL CULTURE AND THE LEFT'S LONG MARCH

GARY MARKS

The cultural-left's march through the institutions originated from social science and humanities departments in Western universities, particularly the United States. Its roots are classical Marxism, critical theory and post-modernism. During the 1970s and 1980s, neo-Marxist and critical theory flourished in the social sciences throughout Western countries until abruptly curtailed by the fall of East European communism. However, many elements of neo-Marxist and critical theory became incorporated into postmodernism. These three theoretical approaches are strongly opposed to capitalism and Western institutions, advocating radical and fundamental changes. They provide the intellectual basis for much of today's extremist political agenda including feminist and gender theories, deep green environmentalism and the global movement to decolonise the curriculum in Western countries.

This chapter will provide short discussions on aspects of these three theoretical approaches relevant to the left's march though the institutions, followed by sections on academia, what students 'learn' at university and the left's political agenda.

Traditional and Neo Marxism

The premises of classical Marxism are as follows. The bourgeoisie own and control the means of production and appropriate the surplus value of wage labourers, the proletariat. Surplus value is the difference between the value of workers' productive output and their costs. The third Marxist class is the petty bourgeoisie comprised of farmers with small holdings, shopkeepers, the self-employed and small business owners. According to classical Marxism, the contradictions inherent within capitalism will eventually lead to its demise. With increased capitalist development: real wages fall (immiseration); capitalist modes of production further permeate society (e.g. undermining the petty bourgeoisie) increasing the size of the proletariat (proletarianisation); and capitalists increase their share of the economic surplus at the expense of workers increasing economic inequality (polarisation).

Together immiseration, proletarianisation and polarisation will transform the working class from a 'class in itself' to a 'class for itself' and socialist revolution would ensue overthrowing the bourgeoisie. The working class in capitalist societies, a 'class in itself', experiences false consciousness because it is unaware of its exploitation by the capitalist class. In contrast, the working class achieves class consciousness when it realises its oppression under capitalism and the viability of socialist alternatives.

According to Marxist theory the relations of production (between the bourgeoisie and the proletariat) form the economic infrastructure or base. The superstructure provides cultural and ideological supports for the base. The superstructure includes every aspect of society including politics, law, education, religion, the family and the media. The superstructure is both a product of, and provides support for, the base.

Marxism is a philosophy and an explanatory theory of history. Dialectical materialism originated from philosophy, emphasising the primacy of material conditions over ideology, reversing Hegel's conflict of ideas. The material world exists independently of the perceptions of human beings. What shapes human society are the means of production (e.g. land, factories, anything that produces wealth) and the relations of production (the bourgeoisie own and control the means of production and the proletariat do not). Under socialism the state would own and control economic production, distribution, and exchange but under communism the state would whither way. Marx and Engels viewed their theory as scientific akin to scientific progress in the natural sciences. Once the theoretical issues are sorted out, Marxists can then engage in political action or praxis.

Historical materialism provides an explanation for the evolution of society from hunter-gatherer societies, ancient societies, feudalism, capitalism and eventually socialism. (There was an additional category of the Asiatic mode of production.) Each type of society has a distinctive infrastructure and superstructure. For example, honour and loyalty were ideologies that supported feudalism but are irrelevant to capitalism. Transformation from one epoch to the next was caused by class conflict. For example, capitalism arose as the bourgeoisie usurped the feudal aristocracy.

In response to Marx and Engels' historical materialism, Weber, a German sociologist writing in the 1920s, argued the transition from feudalism to capitalism was not only due to class conflict but there was an important ideological component. Protestantism, particularly Calvinism, involved a range of ideologies and attitudes conducive to capitalism: the pursuit of profit as virtuous; delayed gratification; hard work; the accumulation of wealth for investment, and good deeds. Weber coined the term 'instrumental rationality', defined as rational actions in pursuit of desired ends which is characteristic of capitalism. Much of Weber's work was concerned with the increasing penetration of 'rationality' in modern societies replacing traditional norms and values, religion, and family and group loyalties as motivators of human behaviour.

Workers in capitalist society are alienated because they are only part of the production process. In contrast, artisans are not alienated because that have full control of production from conception to completion. Alienation occurs as a result of the stratified class system; it estranges workers from other human beings. Since work is fundamental to human beings, workers in capitalist production are divorced from their 'species being'. These Marxist ideas resonate with elements of the contemporary environmental movements in that modern society has estranged people from the natural world (the Gaia) and from their humanness which is 'natural' and good.

Another important element of Marxist theory is the concept of hegemony. The term was originally used by Lenin advocating hegemonic control of society after the revolution, so that the 'guidance' provided by the communist party could not be easily challenged. The Italian communist Antonio Gramsci, who wrote during the 1920s and 1930s, applied the concept of hegemony to capitalist societies. He argued that the bourgeoisie propagated its own values and ideologies throughout society, so that they become common sense obscuring realistic socialist alternatives. For example, feminists drawing on Gramsci condemn capitalist societies as patriarchal on the basis women are conditioned to be feminine and subservient to men.

He proposed a strategy whereby the intelligentsia fights capitalist hegemony by educating workers to promote class consciousness. The neo-Marxists of the 1970s and 1980s also believed in hegemony. According to the neo-Marxist philosopher Louis Althusser, the power of the ruling class was maintained by Ideological State Apparatuses (ISAs) including: the education system, the media, the Church, even sporting clubs. Althusser distinguished ISAs from the Repressive State Apparatuses (RSAs) comprising the Police, the Armed forces, and the law.

Since the 19th century Marxists have argued that the traditional nuclear family is important to the preservation of capitalism. It provides the mechanism for the inheritance of wealth, is the primary unit of consumption in capitalism, a bastion of private property, and a private institution insulated from the public sphere and political action. It promotes ideologies supportive of capitalist social relations such as respect for authority and obedience. It subordinates women and children. In families, women perform the labour of maintaining their working-class husbands and raising the next generation of workers for free.

Nineteenth century Marxists, including Engels, would commonly advocate the abolition of the family and matrimony, communal care of children and freer sexual relationships. Marxist analysis of the family is the basis of modern Marxist feminism. Modern activists are aware of the theoretical importance of the family to maintain capitalism so seek to undermine the family through their advocacy of non-traditional relationships such as same sex marriage. Activists' disdain for Christianity but tolerance for non-Western religions can be traced to idea that Western religions maintain capitalist social relations.

Education features prominently in neo-Marxist analyses as the primary mechanism for class reproduction. The norms and values working class students learn at school (e.g. respect for authority, obedience) are the same norms and values that facilitate their exploitation by future capitalist employers. In contrast, middle-class students are taught independence, self-control and leadership. The idea that success at school is due to ability and hard work is dismissed as a false meritocratic ideology propagated by the ruling class.

The most prominent Marxist analysis of education is Bourdieu's cultural capital theory. Economically privileged children become inculcated with elite culture (serious literature, plays, classical music, ballet, opera, the fine arts) which is the same culture that underlies education systems. Therefore, students from privileged backgrounds will naturally be far more successful than other students because of their superior cultural understanding.

Neo-Marxist ideas on the importance of social class and socioeconomic background for educational outcomes dominates both educational research and policy in Western countries. A good example is the Gonski model which cites cultural capital and class inequality to justify its funding model. A model based on the belief that additional funding, instead of a more rigorous curriculum and evidence-based teaching practices, will lead to higher standards and improved outcomes.

The Russian revolutionaries Lenin and Trotsky extended Marxist analysis to the relationship between the West and the rest of the world. The general argument was that the bourgeoisie of Western countries exploited their colonies by cheaply appropriating their natural resources and labour and by cornering local consumer markets to the detriment of local producers. Here race can be included into Marxist analysis since the exploited colonies were almost invariably non-European.

In Australia, there are Marxist analyses of how Indigenous people were co-opted into capitalist social relations by wage labour to their detriment. After World War II, dependency and world systems theories replaced colonialisation theory. According to these theories, especially postcolonial theory, the economic relationships between Western countries and developing countries benefit the former at the expense of the latter. A world socialist government would redistribute resources fairly.

Critical theory and the Frankfurt school

Critical theory is a 20th century reconstruction of Marxism which originated with the Frankfurt school—a school of social theory and critical philosophy—established in Germany in 1923. After the rise of Hitler, it moved briefly to Switzerland and then to the United States. 'Theory' is somewhat of a misnomer; it is not theory in the sense of accounting for empirical observations, but a critique of Western society and its institutions designed to promote revolutionary understanding. According to Marcuse, critical theory analyses capitalist society in the light of its capabilities for improving the human condition.

Habermas maintained that critical theory is emancipatory, building on the unfinished business of the Enlightenment. Liberation involves liberation from both economic and psychological oppression, so critical theory was as much concerned with psychoanalysis and Freud, as with capitalism and Marx. More generally, Frankfurt school's critiques were focused not just on capitalism, but on all aspects of Western civilisation. In contrast to classical Marxism and neo-Marxism, critical theory does not make predictions and generate falsifiable hypotheses.

The motivation of the Frankfurt school was, in part, a response to the dismal prospects for proletariat revolutions in advanced capitalist countries. Marxists were disillusioned by the failure of the attempted socialist 1919 revolution in Germany and other attempted revolutions in Europe. The 1917 Russian revolution did not fit into Marxist logic; achieved by a political coup d'état in a largely agricultural society. The Marxist predictions of immiseration and polarisation were not realised as workers in industrialised countries were not interested in storming the barricades as they had higher standards of living in the 1920s than they did in the 1840s.

In classical Marxism, the state was understood as a committee run by the bourgeoisie for managing the common affairs of the bourgeoisie. The Frankfurt school conceived the state as more powerful and autonomous compared to what classical Marxism argued. It was a major reason for the absence of working-class revolutionary movements since it had effectively abolished the fundamental contradiction between capital and labour. The state passed laws to the benefit of workers and through taxation transferred wealth from the bourgeoisie to the proletariat forestalling the processes of immiseration, proletarianisation and polarisation.

Poultanzas argued that state was undertheorised, and the state was instrumental in preserving capitalism by creating alliances between naturally opposed classes such as President Franklin D. Roosevelt's New Deal undermining the proletariat's revolutionary potential. For both neo-Marxists and critical theorists, control of the state and its ISAs and RSAs is fundamental to transitioning to socialism.

Critical theorists were very critical of popular culture—novels, radio, recorded music, film and television—and identified it as another instrument for economic and political control, crushing individuality in much the same way as artisans were crushed by capitalist mass production. Entertainment and sport were considered 'manipulated pleasures'. Marcuse extended the hegemony argument to consumerism. Rising affluence had obscured the truly exploitative nature of capitalism. Marcuse argued availability of consumer items in increasingly wealthy Western countries—refrigerators, vacuum cleaners, washing machines—was not liberating but simply another form of hegemonic social control. These ideas persist in contemporary critiques of materialism, consumerism and commercialism best illustrated by the deep green environmental movement.

Critical theory argued that family as an institution was full of contradictions, between authority and love, individual and group identities, and women's control of domestic labour and their subordination. They reiterated the argument that the family was an important bulwark for capitalism. Horkheimer linked the patriarchy of the family to the rise of European fascism. Some of the political advocacy on domestic violence can be traced to Marxist analyses of the family.

Horkheimer extended Weber's concept of instrumental rationality arguing it too contributes to capitalist oppression. Capitalist economies and state bureaucracies rely on deliberate planning of means to an end. Aspects of instrumental rationality, quantification, abstraction, and bureaucratisation also contributed to alienation. 'Rationality' which propels efficiency and growth in capitalist economies, is itself irrational because productivity is destructive of the free development of human needs and faculties. Critical theorists did not consider that increased rationalisation led to increased productivity which in turn increased prosperity. Critical theorists have little to say about how prosperity is generated through markets and other forms of exchange. Importantly markets decentralise power, providing individuals with the freedom to choose. As a philosophical school concerned with liberating humans from oppression, it is odd they are opposed to markets.

Instrumental rationality is part of critical theory's critique of science. Science creates the false reality of scientific progress for the good of all. This contrasts with classical Marxism that was impressed with the transformative potential of science for a more humane society. Marx and Engels understood their analyses as scientific. The neo-Marxist Carchedi dismissed the idea that knowledge is apolitical and argued that scientific knowledge is capitalist class knowledge whose purpose is exploitation of the working class to increase profit.

Critical school theorists critiqued positivism for its faith in science as a progressive force in human history, and the extension of its methods and emphasis on objectivity were not appropriate for the social sciences. The Frankfurt school also argued capitalist societies used science to dominate nature; a theme adopted by environmentalists of later generations. On environment issues, environmentalists are much less critical of socialist and non-Western countries like China and in the 1970s and 1980s the USSR.

The argument that science is political was further developed by postmodernists. Nowadays, science is no longer regarded as politically neutral—as it was it the 1950s and 1960s. Ironically, science is far more politicised today than it was in the 1960s and 1970s illustrated by postcolonial activists arguing Western science is guilty of imperialism and white supremacism.

The left's march through the institutions originated with the Frankfurt school. Critical theorists were continually disappointed with the lack of revolutionary zeal among the working classes of Western countries. Even in 1971, despite the tumultuous events of the late 1960s, and over a century of careful theoretical work by critical theorists and other Marxists, the prospects of socialist revolutions in Western countries were dimmer than they were in the early 1920s. The idea of the march through the institutions originated with one of Marcuse's students.

Marcuse agreed that the long march through the institutions, referencing Mao's long march, was the only effective way of overthrowing capitalism. Revolutionaries and their proxies would work against institutions while working for them rather than waiting for the proletariat to become a class-for-itself. Obviously, the long march was never formally organised but involves activists promoting left wing causes and ideas and employing like-minded people.

Habermas argued that the ideological support bases of capitalism were being eroded, evidenced by the growth of the counterculture and the anti-war, youth dominated movement of the 1960s. He argued that capitalism was undergoing a legitimation crisis since its fundamental norms and values were constantly attacked.

Since the 1970s critiques of Western society have been so unrelenting and persuasive that sizable proportions of Western citizens indicate they support socialism which is naively understood as simply about social justice and equality, disregarding the economic and political disasters of socialist states over the last century. Indeed, Western civilisation is facing a legitimation crisis but not from radicalised youth movements but from within its various institutions.

Postmodernism

Postmodernism rejects the fundaments of normal science, objectivity, deductive and inductive reasoning, and falsification. Postmodernism contends that science and its methods should not enjoy a privileged status vis-à-vis other ways of knowing. Their rejection of science is far more radical than critical theory's critique of positivism. There is no objective reality independent of human perception. Reality is socially constructed by political and economic factors with the intent of preserving power structures. Language is the primary basis for the social construction of reality. The criterion for establishing the truth of statements is not correspondence with empirical observations. There are 'truths' but they pertain to particular social contexts and social groups. Similarly, there are 'theories' for particular social groups which are activistic rather than explanatory.

The task of postmodernism is to deconstruct language and expose the unequal power structures that are oppressing minorities specifically women, people of colour and LBGTIQ+ communities. Class is not forgotten but relegated to one dimension of power and oppression along with gender and race. Other dimensions (e.g. sexuality) are added depending on the context. Intersectionality occurs when two or more dimensions overlap.

Postmodernism has several commonalties with Marxism and critical theory. Like Marxism and critical theory, postmodernism is concerned with social inequalities and liberation from oppressive power structures associated with capitalism and Western civilisation. The malevolent role of social institutions—the state, the education and political systems, the family, religion, the mass media—and culture in maintaining the inequitable social order are left largely intact. All agree that the inequalities in Western societies are profound and enduring; they can only be addressed by revolutionary change.

All three political philosophies have little sympathy for opposing political views or core values of Western countries, for example freedom of expression, equality before the law, the separation of powers or democracy. Each contends that the many and profound ills of Western societies can only be solved if revolutionaries assume total control of all economic, political and cultural institutions.

There are many differences between postmodernism and both Marxism and critical theory. In contrast to Marxism, there is no overarching philosophy akin to dialectical materialism and no privileged status for Marxism or psychoanalysis. The dominance of the material relations of production in neo-Marxism and critical theory has been replaced by the neo-Hegelian idea of conflict between oppressive and liberating ideologies. Similarly, postmodernism has no over-arching historical explanation for the development of the modern world.

Postmodernism is uninterested in what makes societies prosperous and believe society's resources should be distributed not by markets but by political criteria. The villains are no longer the bourgeoisie and capitalism but men, whites, Christians, neoliberals and conservatives. The Enlightenment is not viewed as positively by postmodernist as by Marxists or critical theorists.

Academia

The Vietnam war, the Paris riots in 1968 and the 1960s counterculture produced a revival in classical Marxism and critical theory. Universities were expanding, and Marxism became a respected academic tradition in many social science departments. There were self-identified Marxists in economics, sociology, education, history, law, geography, architecture, anthropology, literature and psychology. Marxist orientated courses were popular among students encouraging faculties to replace conservative and centre-left academics with neo-Marxists.

A sizable proportion of self-identified neo-Marxists genuinely believed that Western societies had entered the late capitalist phase of economic development and economic collapse was inevitable. They viewed their intellectual contributions as important for the transition to socialism, part of the revolution's vanguard. Reagan and Thatcher were understood, not as a revival of neoliberalism, but as symptomatic of the crisis enveloping capitalism. Others simply enjoyed their high paid tenured positions, fame in a circumscribed world and access to students.

The 1970s and the 1980s were the golden age of neo-Marxism. There were academic debates on many aspects of Marxism: the transition from feudalism to capitalism; false consciousness and hegemony; proletarianisation (of lower white-collar workers); embourgeoisement (of well-paid skilled manual workers), the separation of ownership from control of the means of production (the rise of the managerial class), the labour theory of (surplus) value, commodification, alienation and strange concepts such as commodity fetishism and reification. In addition, the totality of Marxist theory meant that every aspect of society could be subject to Marxist analysis.

These debates rarely referenced empirical data. The preferred methodology was hermeneutics which was originally concerned with interpreting the Bible and had been extensively used in the study of Plato, Aristotle's works and other prominent texts. Debates would involve interpretation of Marxist texts to ascertain what was really meant followed by, sometimes repeated, critique and reinterpretation. Debates were seldom resolved because there is always room for further interpretation and critique.

Furthermore, English-speaking academics were at a disadvantage since they had to rely on translations leading to the creation of a bilingual caste that could interpret the revered texts just like priests. These activities had all the characteristics of normal science: seminars, conferences, journal articles, scholarly books, research grants and PhD students. However, this enterprise was not scientific, arguing about the finer points of Marxist theory was akin to tedious theological debates within a well-defined belief system. It is difficult to argue that all this scholarly activity was at all beneficial to anyone except those drawing salaries. The opportunity costs are probably substantial.

Neo-Marxism was dealt a severe blow with the 1989 collapse of communism in Eastern Europe and two years later in the Soviet Union. Academic Marxism's implicit assumption that socialism is desirable became even more untenable since the only successful popular uprisings of the 20th century were against socialist governments in 1989. The once dominant communist and socialist parties of Western Europe had lost much popular support.

In the 1950s, it was possible to compare East and West Germany, Austria and Hungary, North and South Korea, even the US and the USSR and extoll the superiority of socialist systems in terms of health, education, housing, welfare, women's rights and even standards of living. By the 1990s this was not at all possible. Socialism had not delivered economic prosperity, equality or basic human rights and many socialist states were, at times, dystopian nightmares.

The neo-Marxist 'project' had been unravelling well before the early 1990s. Class has outlived its usefulness as an explanatory concept. Empirically, it was increasingly apparent that class was a weak or declining predictor of attitudes and values, and political and ideological orientations. One brave academic in urban studies likened social class to the emperor with no clothes. There was no consensus on the class structure of modern societies since many occupational groups—technicians, professionals, managers and state employees—could not be unambiguously assigned to the bourgeoisie or proletariat.

The petty bourgeoisie was not destroyed by further capitalist development. The rise of capitalism from feudalism could not simply be attributed to class conflict. Dependency and world-system theories could not account for the economic rise of Japan, the Asian tigers and later China; and countries less integrated with world capitalism tended to be poorer. Institutions and governance provide more compelling explanations for national prosperity. However, for much of academia the radical transformative agenda was not abandoned; neo-Marxists and critical theorists simply adopted postmodernism. Prominent neo-Marxists of the 1980s become post-modernists in the 1990s. Similarly, critical theory influenced by postmodernism morphed into a variety of academic fields purportedly about liberation from oppression, for example, feminist, queer, black, trans and postcolonial theories.

Postmodernist scholarship typically involves taking one aspect of contemporary society and deconstructing relevant materials (mainly texts) with obligatory deference to theorists from the pantheon of postmodernists (e.g. Baudrillard, Derrida, Foucault, Lyotard). Ironically, the pantheon is comprised almost entirely of white European men. Every aspect and cultural product of Western civilisation is fair game for postmodernist deconstruction and each is found contributing to victimhood and oppression.

Like academic Marxism, few academics are thoroughly versed in the revered texts because the language is unintelligible, but their impenetrability only adds to their credibility. Postmodernism is a political ideology again with many religious characteristics. There is a fundamental and unquestioned belief in the existence of oppressive power structures. Its contentions are not subject to falsification. Like neo-Marxism in its heyday, these activities had all the hallmarks of research in the hard sciences, but its legitimacy is based on political ideology not science.

The standards of postmodern scholarship are so low that it is easy to fool editors if the text is sufficiently 'postmodern'. Examples are Sokal's 1996 *Toward a Transformative Hermeneutics of Quantum Gravity* and seven hoax articles recently published in academic journals on topics such as 'Queer Performativity in Urban Dog Parks' and combatting transphobia by sex toy use. In 1998 Sokal published a book attacking postmodernism as fashionable nonsense and an abuse of science.

However, postmodernism in the social sciences continues to grow even in the most prestigious institutions. In *Cynical Theories*, Pluckrose and Lindsay describe postmodernist theory and activism as anti-Enlightenment, dangerous and authoritarian. They argue the unchecked penetration of postmodernist 'scholarship' threatens liberal democracy and Western civilisation. The irony is that capitalism and Western civilisation, the foil of Marxist, critical theory and postmodernist attacks, has produced unprecedented prosperity which allows these destructive ideas to permeate.

The most serious problem for academic research in the humanities and social sciences is the rejection of basic scientific principles. Objectivity is rejected as important by both critical theory and postmodernism. Since there is no such thing as objectivity, scholars are free to promote their own personal political and ideological orientations as scholarship and tailor research findings to political agendas. The criteria for evaluating research has become unashamedly politicalised. One of Merton's norms of science is universalism, the irrelevance of researchers' personal characteristics and orientations.

For neo-Marxism and critical theory, political orientations are important in evaluating scholarship. For postmodernism personal characteristics are paramount. Detached scepticism, another of Merton's norms of science, is no longer respected. Instead, prominent publications that support the dominate narrative, for example Piketty's *Capital in the Twenty-First Century* or Wilkinson and Pickett's *The Spirit Level* are lauded. Publications that question the dominant narratives are attacked and their authors vilified (e.g. Herrnstein and Murray's *The Bell Curve*) sometimes by respected academics (e.g. the noble prize-winning economist James Heckman).

A major problem with dismissing objectivity is that evidence becomes much less relevant to policy. It does not matter how many studies show girl's and women's outcomes have improved, and that in education, superior to that of men and boys, the narrative of systematic and structural sexism remains. Similarly, despite overwhelming evidence for the importance of ability and genetics in education, socioeconomic status and social class explanations dominate. In Western countries, where there is available data, overt racism has declined. Narratives on white privilege and systemic racism vilify, or at least ignore, the predominately white working class of Western countries that Marxist theory was aiming to liberate. There is little evidence of ethnic discrimination in Australia. Second generation immigrants do as well or better than the Australian born. Such evidence is irrelevant to the multicultural industry.

It is now well-established that prosperity can be largely attributed to the free exchange of ideas and goods; the presence of markets rather than government directive; minimal corruption and inclusive rather than extractive regimes. (Extractive regimes exploit a country's resources for the benefit of a small elite supported by RSAs; inclusive regimes more equitably distribute resources throughout society.) In other words, Western capitalism. However, the policy prescription from the UN and other international agencies is mainly about redistribution justified by the tired rhetoric of neo-Marxist theories.

Students

As a result of cultural-left theories university curriculums in the humanities and social science have been incrementally radicalised, with the notable exceptions of economics and psychology. Journalist students learn that the media is an important element of the superstructure and impartiality and balance are bourgeois concepts. Student teachers learn about cultural capital theory and other theories that explain how education and schools perpetuate socioeconomic inequalities. Social work students learn that most of the social problems they will experience as professionals can be attributed to capitalism or the oppressive nature of Western cultural institutions.

Political science students encounter social class as an explanation for political behaviour and world capitalism to explain the relationships between countries. Students learn about the nefarious behaviour of Western countries, especially the United States. First year sociology students are asked to compare Marx and Weber's accounts of the rise of capitalism. History students are taught themes such as colonisation, resistance and socialism, ignoring the chronology of events. Many young people are unaware of the importance of Greco-Roman and Judeo-Christian legacies, the renaissance and the reformation, the Enlightenment, and the industrial revolution to present day society.

English students focus on deconstruction, and the political and socioeconomic context of a work of literature not its content or ideas. Women's studies contrast Marxist feminist and radical feminist perspectives. The holy trinity of class, race and gender feature prominently in many social science subjects. Students are often asked to read very difficult neo-Marxist and postmodernist source material. The pervasiveness of radical approaches to the humanities and social sciences borders on hegemonic, few alternatives are presented, if they are (e.g. neoliberalism) it's only to be parodied, deconstructed and rejected. Of course, for most students the political messaging does not penetrate very much, but they realise that to pass they need to at least pay lip service to one or more radical analyses.

Politics

Historically, political movements aiming to take power loudly assert society is facing an unprecedented crisis and the only way the crisis can be resolved is for them to take control. The so-called carbon induced climate emergency is a contemporary manifestation of this tactic. There have been many 'crises' over the last 50 years: economic inequality, peak oil, overpopulation, mass starvation and in the 1960s global cooling. All these crises were promoted by the left exaggerating the extent of the crisis, all blame capitalism and all propose similar neo-Marxist solutions involving government control and redistribution.

The march through the institutions has been amazingly successful. Organisations that were once a bit to the left—the ABC, the BBC, CNN, MSBC, the UN, the *Guardian*, universities—have moved further left. Organisations that were firmly centre-right—the OECD, the *Economist* and *Time* magazines, the World Bank, the IMF, medical organisations such as the AMA, Australian commercial TV, the armed forces, the police—are now typically on the left. The same is true of corporations that were once bastions of capitalism and conservative values. Organisations that were once generally apolitical—the AFL, the NRL, the NBA in the US—now promote left wing causes.

Even formerly apolitical magazines—*Scientific American*, *Vanity Fair*, *Teen Vogue*—have now joined the chorus of left-wing voices. The bulk of the media and social media (e.g. Facebook, Twitter, Slate, Politco) are now also ashamedly left-wing and no longer try to hide their political biases. The link between Black Lives Matter (BLM) and the neo-Marxist group Antifa, for example, is ignored with BLM described simply as an anti-racist movement and not one committed to a violent, destructive agenda.

Citizens at home and in their workplaces are continually exposed to extremist political views. But, as they are packaged in non-threatening language including social justice, equality and progressive politics, the public is unaware that many of the issues are underpinned by neo-Marxism, critical theory and post-modernism. While the election of conservative governments in Australia and the United Kingdom indicate that the radical left has not been wholly successful, the aphorism 'the price of freedom is eternal vigilance' should never be forgotten.

The militant left never sleeps and their totalitarian agenda must be vigorously opposed by those who value Western civilisation, the ideals of the Enlightenment and the benefits capitalism continues to provide.

Gary N. Marks is an honorary principal fellow in the Department of Sociology, Social and Political Sciences at the University of Melbourne. He has a PhD in Sociology and has been employed at the University of Queensland, the Australian National University, the Australian Council for Educational Research and the University of Melbourne. His publications are in four main areas: education (student achievement, university entrance performance, school completion and early school leaving, school effects), labour market outcomes (e.g. employment, unemployment, occupational attainment, occupational mobility, income and wealth) and social outcomes (e.g. well-being, leaving home and family formation). His book Education, Social Background and Cognitive: The Decline of the Social *(Routledge, 2014) is about the importance of cognitive ability and education, and the declining importance of social background for social stratification.*

SCHOOL EDUCATION

KEVIN DONNELLY

The philosophy of the school room in one generation will be the philosophy of the government in the next.
Abraham Lincoln, 16th President of the United States of America.

As argued by Abraham Lincoln, what happens in a nation's schools has a dramatic and far-reaching impact on society as students are future citizens who will decide who governs, what policies are implemented and how society is shaped.

One of the primary ways the cultural-left has been able to impose its politically correct ideology on Western societies, including Australia, is by taking control of schools and influencing what is taught, how students are assessed and how teachers and students interact in the classroom.

While young people are influenced by family, peers, social networking sites and the broader media it's their school experience that sets the foundation for how they live their lives, inter-act with others, the careers and professions they follow and how they relate to the broader society and the world in general.

To parents with school age children and the broader public it's obvious education has become a casualty of what is often described as the culture wars. A struggle, as noted by the British conservative politician Michael Gove in *Celsius 7/7*, that began with Germany's Frankfurt School in the 1920s when Marxist inspired academics shifted their campaign 'away from economic arguments and towards cultural ones'.

As a result of the cultural-left's success in winning the culture wars, instead of being impartial and balanced and the curriculum being centred on the pursuit of knowledge, wisdom and truth, education is being used to indoctrinate students with politically correct language, ideology and group think.

One example is the neo-Marxist inspired Safe Schools gender fluidity program that teaches primary and secondary age students that girls can be boys and boys can be girls; and compared to being lesbian, gay, bisexual, transgender, intersex, queer or plus (LGBTIQ+) there's nothing preferable or beneficial about heterosexuality. A second example involves the Australian Education Union encouraging students to wag school and take strike action over climate change and a third is the way the curriculum undermines the strengths and benefits of Western civilisation by promoting multiculturalism and cultural relativism.

Students are also taught to believe all men are misogynists and that societies like Australia are riven with structural sexism and unconscious bias against women and girls. Despite their rights to full citizenship and the billions spent every year on Aboriginal services and welfare, students are taught society is awash with structural racism and the arrival of the First Fleet represents an invasion leading to genocide.

Instead of competition and rewarding students based on ability and merit they are told everyone deserves success and it is wrong to have winners and losers. Instead of providing a ladder of opportunity where concentration, hard work and commitment lead to academic success students are told the education system is inequitable and unjust where wealthy, privileged Catholic and Independent school students are always unfairly advantaged.

In literature, instead of encountering those enduring novels, plays, poems and short stories that say something profound about human nature and the world in which we live, students are taught to deconstruct and analyse texts in terms of power relationships, identity politics and victimhood. In today's postmodern, new-age classroom SMS messaging, graffiti, movie posters and computer games are on the same footing as Shakespeare's plays and the novels of Jane Austen and David Malouf.

Teaching grammar, spelling and syntax has also been jettisoned in favour of free expression and creativity and instead of learning to read based on a phonics and phonemic awareness approach teachers are told to adopt a whole language model based on the mistaken belief that learning to read is as natural as learning to talk. As a result, generations of students, especially boys, are leaving school illiterate and educationally disadvantaged.

Whereas English once involved teaching clear thinking and the importance of logic and reason when evaluating arguments and different points of view as a result of critical theory and postmodernism, students now judge arguments according to how they feel. Postmodernist theory denies words have readily agreed meanings and argues how individuals relate to one another and the wider world is subjective and relative.

As detailed by the American academic Richard Tarnes, those committed to postmodernism believe 'human knowledge is subjectively determined by a multitude of factors; that objective essences, or things-in-themselves, are neither accessible nor positable… The critical search for truth is constrained to be tolerant of ambiguity and pluralism, and its outcome will necessarily be knowledge that is relative and fallible rather than absolute or certain'.

In history, instead of learning about Australia's origins and evolution as a liberal, democratic society and the significance of Western civilisation, including the ongoing debt owed to Judeo-Christianity, teachers are told they must decolonise the curriculum and rid it of European essentialism and white supremacism.

In the Australian National Curriculum teachers are also told they must teach Indigenous science on the basis science is a cultural construct and there is nothing preferable or superior about Western science. In the science classroom throwing boomerangs is considered as great a breakthrough as open heart surgery, allowing planes to stay in the air and putting a man on the moon.

Given the success of the cultural-left's long march students are also taught global warming is man-made, fossil fuels are destroying the planet and the only way to save future generations is to embrace 100 per cent renewables based on unreliable and costly wind farms and solar panels.

During Mao's cultural revolution academics were attacked, universities and schools disrupted, and students turned into Red Guards mindlessly chanting slogans from Mao's *Little Red Book*. In Pol Pot's Cambodia educated people were banished from the cities and forced to work in rural concentration camps and undergo forced re-education. In Hitler's Germany and Stalin's Russia, education, instead of encouraging independent thought and critical awareness, was also captured to ensure totalitarian mind control and group think. While the impact of the cultural-left's long march through the schools and the education system is not as extreme or violent, the underlying rationale and justification are the same.

According to those committed to neo-Marxist inspired critical theory the aim is to overthrow capitalist society by infiltrating and capturing the institutions that underpin and safeguard our way of life. In the words of Joan Kirner, the former Victorian Minister for Education and Premier:

If we are egalitarian in our intention we have to reshape education so that it is part of the socialist struggle for equality, participation and social change, rather than an instrument of the capitalist system.

> **Joan Kirner** (1983) in 'Education – Where From? Where to?'
> Victorian Fabian Society Pamphlet 41.

The Australian Education Union, like minded academics and professional bodies like the Australian Association for the Teachers of English and the Australian Curriculum Studies Association also champion a cultural-left view of education. One where the purpose of education is to radically reshape society and establish the left's utopia by indoctrinating students with politically correct ideology and group think.

A liberal education

*If then we recognize education as an initiation into a civilization,
we may regard it as beginning to learn our way about a material,
emotional, moral and intellectual inheritance, and as learning to
recognize the varieties of human utterance and to participate in the
conversation they compose.*

Michael Oakeshott (1991) 'The study of politics in a university'
in *Rationalism in Politics and Other Essays.*

Before detailing the cultural-left's long march through primary and
secondary schools it's important to understand up until the late 1960s
and early 1970s the approach to education across the English-speaking
world was fundamentally different.

As suggested by the English philosopher Michael Oakeshott and
under the heading of a liberal education the belief is each generation
of students has to become familiar with the unique knowledge,
understanding and skills associated with their particular society
and culture. In Australia's case, notwithstanding we are increasingly
culturally and ethnically diverse, the reality is we are a Western
culture and it is Western civilisation that underpins and informs our
way of life.

While geographically close to Asia, India and the Pacific islands the
reality is much of our culture, way of life and the institutions we take for
granted owe their origins to the United Kingdom, Ireland and Europe.

State and commonwealth political systems are based largely on
a Westminster form of parliamentary government inherited from
England and a legal system based on common law where the judiciary
is independent and citizens have the right to live free of unwarranted
and unjust government intervention and control.

Concepts like freedom of religion, freedom of conscience, freedom of
expression and freedom of assembly plus the right to own property and
to make a profit do not exist in totalitarian China and Putin's Russia or
in Cuba, Venezuela and many African states.

Our language is English and while evolving and becoming more distinctive much of our literature, art, music and dance can only be fully appreciated and understood by acknowledging the debt owed to the United Kingdom and Europe. Shakespeare's plays and Greek tragedies like *Medea*, *Oedipus* and *Antigone*, for example, are unique to Western civilisation.

Australia's origins as a British penal settlement and the fact for most of our history those arriving here came from the United Kingdom, Ireland and Europe also suggests students need to be familiar with key aspects of Western civilisation including significant historical events like the Renaissance, the Reformation, the Enlightenment, the Industrial Revolution and the impact of modernity and post modernity associated with the digital age.

In addition to learning about Western civilisation another significant aspect of a liberal education is that it promotes the ability to think rationally and logically and to weigh evidence free of personal bias and prejudice. What constitutes exemplary art or music, whether a scientific hypothesis is correct or not and whether a mathematical algorism solves a particular problem does not depend on gender, ethnicity, class or race.

In Australia, while we are not a theocracy and there is a division between church and state it's also true as detailed in Larry Siedentop's book *Inventing the Individual: The Origins of Western Liberalism* that Christianity and the New Testament are essential aspects of Western civilisation.

Christ's admonition 'Thou shalt love thy neighbour as thyself' and the belief 'There is neither Jew nor Greek, there is neither bond nor free, there is neither male nor female: for ye are all one in Christ Jesus' heralded a radically different world where all were to be treated equally and not discriminated against.

As such a liberal education is inherently moral in character and while drawing on secular philosophy beginning with the ancient Greeks and the concept of natural law owes much to Christian teachings and beliefs. Concepts such as good and evil, temptation and sin, redemption and absolution, forgiveness and charity infuse much of the West's literature, music, art, law and politics.

Christian parables and Christ's teachings while often not recognised are also an important aspect of the language and expressions we use in our everyday lives. Examples include: turn the other cheek, be a good Samaritan, let he without sin cast the first stone and love thy neighbour as thyself.

The English poet and school inspector Mathew Arnold in *Culture and Anarchy* when detailing the importance of culture argues education should be directed at 'the best which has been thought and said' and that it should also involve 'turning a fresh and free thought upon our stock notions and habits'.

Instead of being ossified and unchanging a liberal education, while acknowledging the past, is also open to evolution and change. In science once accepted orthodoxies are open to revision in the light of new evidence or when they have been proven to be inaccurate. Copernicus when arguing the earth revolved around the sun proved Ptolemy wrong and Albert Einstein revolutionised theories of space and time.

While unpopular in these politically correct times where all students deserve a prize and it is wrong to discriminate it's also true a liberal education is based on meritocracy and the belief not all students have the same ability, motivation or interests. Not all students desire to go to university to study law or medicine and some students are better suited to an apprenticeship or trade.

A liberal education is also based on the assumption learning does not happen intuitively or by accident and that for students to master difficult and complex subjects requires application, concentration and hard work. To learn a foreign language, to play the violin or to master complex algorisms takes years of study and effort.

The cultural-left's long march

In a society disfigured by class exploitation, sexual and racial oppression, and in chronic danger of war and environmental destruction, the only education worth the name is one that forms people capable of taking part in their own liberation.

Connell, Ashenden, Kessler, Dowsett (1982).
Making the Difference Schools, Families and Social Division.

The above quotation is taken from an Australian textbook popular in teacher training courses during the 1980s and exemplifies the cultural-left's rationale for taking control of the education system. According to its critics, a liberal education instead of being beneficial or worthwhile is complicit in reinforcing the inequities and injustices characteristic of Western capitalist, racist and misogynist societies like Australia.

In America similar books including *Schooling in Capitalist America* by Samuel Bowles and Herbert Gintis and Ivan Illich's *Deschooling Society* argued the existing education system needed a radical overhaul as it was guilty of reinforcing capitalist domination and control.

English publications including Michael F.D Young's *Knowledge and Control* and Mandan Sarup's *Marxism and Education* added to the chorus all directed at transforming education and freeing students from the supposed bondage inflicted by an unjust and inequitable society.

Instead of schools being places of learning where students are educated to be knowledgeable, informed and critically aware citizens and able to lead fulfilling lives and find gainful employment the cultural-left champions the belief schools must be used to promote its neo-Marxist inspired ideology.

While the origins of critical theory can be traced back to the *Prison Notebooks* written by the Italian Marxist Antonio Gramsci and the establishment of the Frankfurt School in Germany during the 1920s, the campaign to overthrow capitalist society gained new intensity during the cultural revolution of the late '60s and early '70s.

This was the time of Vietnam moratoriums and the rise of a youth counter-culture movement exemplified by the slogans 'make love not war', 'turn on, tune in, drop out' and 'if it feels good do it'. In response to the early years of the French Revolution the English poet Wordsworth wrote 'Bliss was it in that dawn to be alive! But to be young was very heaven' and the same can be said for those coming of age during the late '60s and early '70s.

Germaine Greer's book *The Female Eunuch* was a best seller and feminists campaigned to free themselves from what they saw as subservience to men and the patriarchy. The birth control pill heralded an era of sexual liberation and the emerging hippy culture as a result of mind-expanding drugs like LSD and marijuana, eastern mysticism and meditation turned its back on Western materialism and consumerism.

At universities in England, America and Australia sit-ins became common place where radicalised students demonstrated against the Vietnam war and what was seen as American imperialist aggression. Revolutionary figures like Chairman Mao, Ho Chi Minh and Che Guevara were idolised as freedom fighters and students and like-minded academics condemned university subjects based on a liberal view of education in favour of one embracing critical theory and cultural-left ideology.

As a result, studying literature no longer involved an analysis and evaluation of those works associated with the literary canon but instead was transformed into cultural studies where texts were deconstructed . and critiqued in terms of power relationships.

History as a subject no longer centred on learning about significant historical events and issues as well as influential figures and the evolution of Western civilisation and the world in general. Instead students were taught what the Melbourne historian Stuart Macintyre in *The History Wars* describes as 'history from below'.

A radical approach drawing on a rainbow alliance of neo-Marxist, gender, queer, feminist and postcolonial theories as well as progressive social movements 'formed around sexuality, race and ethnicity'. Macintyre writes 'In the 1960s and 1970s, critical approaches to Australian history questioned established interpretations of settlement and progress. Historians pursued voices frequently absent from the national narrative'.

Teacher training, in part caused by shifting responsibility from stand-alone colleges to university education faculties, also embraced critical theory where the purpose of education centred on critiquing Western, capitalist society and replacing a liberal education with one directed at emancipation and liberation.

Many of those graduating from university during the '60s and '70s cultural revolution became teachers, academics, politicians and public servants and it should not surprise they carried with them the convictions and beliefs imbibed during their undergraduate days. As noted by Michael Gove in *Celsius 7/7*, 'the Left became more and more a movement of those public-sector professionals alerted to cultural issues during their university years, who were on a perpetual quest for new victims onto whom they could project their need to feel righteous anger'.

The Victorian Secondary Teachers Association and the Australian Teachers' Federation (both since renamed the Australian Education Union) were and still are at the vanguard of the cultural-left's campaign to take control. While presenting itself as a professional body directed at advocating and safeguarding the industrial rights of teachers, the union since its inception has promulgated a radical educational agenda.

According to the Australian Education Union (AEU) Australian society is riven with injustice and inequality and concepts like competition and meritocracy plus the academic curriculum reinforce the disadvantage suffered by various victim groups, including: girls, non-English speaking migrants, working class students and those identifying as LGBTIQ+.

Instead of equality of opportunity where students are given an equal chance to succeed as a result of attending well-resourced schools with a rigorous curriculum and well trained, motivated and effective teachers, the AEU champions equality of outcomes and positive discrimination.

As a result, the teacher union has a long history of opposing literacy and numeracy tests including the National Assessment Program Literacy and Numeracy (NAPLAN) and high-risk examinations like the Higher School Certificate based on the belief wealthy privileged non-government school students have an unfair advantage over students in government schools.

While Australia's mainstream political parties support funding Catholic and Independent schools, on the basis all parents pay taxes and have the right to choose where their children go to school, the AEU's policy is to stop funding non-government schools. The union contends such funding unfairly supports society's wealthy elites and denies equality of outcomes where all, regardless of background, ability or motivation, deserve success.

Over the last 20 to 30 years the AEU has urged teachers and students to oppose Australia's involvement in the Iraqi war, denounced the election of conservative governments led by John Howard and argued the school curriculum must embrace the Safe Schools gender fluidity program and a deep green view of climate change and the impending ecological disaster.

The Australian Association for the Teaching of English is the national body representing English teachers and it also for many years has advocated a cultural-left view of education and the purpose of schools. The AATE has especially criticised and undermined the approach to teaching English associated with a liberal education.

The South American Marxist Paulo Freire suggests the purpose of teaching students to read and write is to encourage them to embrace revolutionary change. Drawing on the concept of critical literacy, Freire writes students must be empowered 'to perceive themselves in dialectical relationship with their social reality (and) to assume an increasingly critical attitude toward the world and so to transform it'.

Over the last 40 years the AATE has switched the emphasis from teaching grammar, spelling, punctuation and syntax to championing Freire's concept of critical literacy arguing English teachers have a responsibility to empower and liberate students by teaching them to analyse language and texts through a politically correct prism involving gender, ethnicity, race and class.

Not surprisingly, generations of students have left school with poor spelling skills, unable to punctuate a sentence and ignorant of the parts of speech and how to parse a sentence. Australian students are ranked below 21 other countries in the Progress in International Reading

Study (PIRLS) and ranked 16th in the literacy section of the Programme for International Student Assessment test (PISA). It's not unusual for teachers responsible for teaching a foreign language like French, German or Italian to complain how their task has been made so much more time consuming and difficult because students are illiterate.

As a result of critical literacy classic fairy tales like *Cinderella* and *Snow White and the Seven Dwarfs* are condemned as promoting a heterosexual view of relationships where women are subservient to men and tales like *Little Black Sambo* banished for being racist. *Thomas the Tank Engine* is also targeted by the cultural-left thought police as it apparently reinforces a capitalist-imposed hierarchy.

Literature that has stood the test of time, is moral in character and has something profound and significant to say about human nature and the world in which we live has also been targeted. As a result Shakespeare's *Othello* is deconstructed in terms of Marxist and feminist theories and Conrad's *Heart of Darkness* in terms of postcolonial theory.

In addition to critical literacy the AATE also champions radical LGBTIQ+ gender theory and criticises the English classroom for being guilty of promoting a heteronormative, binary and patriarchal view of gender and sexuality. One example involves the AATE urging classroom teachers to use the gender-neutral pronoun 'they' instead of 'he' and 'she'.

A second example involves an edition of the AATE's journal *English in Australia* (Volume 53, No 2) titled 'Love in English' where, after welcoming same-sex marriage being legalised, teachers are told the subject is guilty of normalising traditional views about gender and sexuality and ignoring the needs of LGBTIQ+ people.

As evidence, one of the chapters in the AATE journal, after investigating the texts set for the national curriculum's senior school English course, concludes the majority of the texts chosen unfairly privilege 'heterosexual and cisgender identities as the norms against which to define the other'.

Such is the AATE's commitment to cultural-left ideology that after

John Howard's conservative government was re-elected in 2004 the editor of the AATE's journal Wayne Sawyer argued teachers had failed to teach critical literacy as so many young people had apparently failed to vote the correct way.

George Orwell, the author of *1984* and *Animal Farm*, believes if citizens are to be critically informed and independently minded, able to resist propaganda and indoctrination, it's crucial they have a firm command of the language and can weigh arguments rationally and logically. Orwell writes 'If thought corrupts language, language can also corrupt thought'.

While not suggesting it's intentional, as a result of the AATE's policies generations of students are leaving school barely literate and as a consequence unaware of and unable to resist language employed to indoctrinate and persuade. Even worse, as a result of abandoning what use to be called clear thinking in senior school English classes, reason and rationality have given way to feelings and emotions when evaluating differing opinions and arguments. Instead of 'I think therefore I am' current generations of young people follow the mantra 'I feel, therefore I am right'.

The Australian Curriculum Studies Association is yet another peak professional body that advocates a cultural-left view of schools and their relationship to the broader society. Established in 1983 ACSA describes itself as 'broadly based educational association supporting the professional interests of educators in curriculum work from all levels and sectors within and beyond Australia'. The national body made up principally of academics and representatives of subject associations describes its purpose as supporting 'curriculum reform informed by the principles of social justice and equity and respect for the democratic rights of all'.

Noble ideals and uncontroversial in themselves but a closer examination of ACSA's publications and initiatives illustrates how the organisation defines education through a politically correct prism. One drawing on critical theory and opposition to a liberal view of education and the purpose of schooling.

Evidence that ACSA is far from impartial and even handed can be found in the publication *Going Public: Education policy and public education in Australia* published in 1998. Authors including Allan Luke, Alan Reid, Sharon Burrow, Jane Kenway and Bob Connell all advocate a centre-left ideology. Not surprisingly the editors describe the book as 'an unashamedly partisan book' dedicated to defending 'social democratic values at the heart of progressive aspirations about public education'.

The chapter on the literacy debate, notwithstanding the widespread evidence that too many students leave school unable to properly read and write, argues the crisis is a manufactured one promoted by critics who are 'alarmist and negative'. Instead of being genuinely concerned about literacy governments are guilty of fabricating a crisis 'to deflect attention away from material problems such as youth poverty and unemployment'.

Instead of conservative governments wanting to help disadvantaged students the argument is liberal politicians are 'part of the dominant cultural groups' seeking 'to organise and regulate the lives and learning of the disadvantaged and subaltern groups'. The definition of literacy put forward in this chapter is one inspired by critical theory, 'one where in a postmodern, postcolonial globalised world' literacy must be empowering and liberating.

A second chapter in the ACSA book, not unexpectedly given its partisan nature, presents a case against funding Catholic and Independent schools as non-government schools embody an approach to education that fosters 'competition, ultra-individualism, growing inequalities, and the partial breakdown of social solidarity and inclusiveness'.

The ACSA book finishes by detailing a strategy directed at taking control of school education to ensure its cultural-left, progressive ideology is implemented. After condemning those critical of multiculturalism, immigration and Indigenous reconciliation the concluding chapter refers to the need to counter what is described as 'reactionary policy development that has fanned deep-seated prejudices, hatreds and fears that obviously lurk beneath the cosmopolitan veneer of Australian society'.

In 2014 I co-chaired the review of the Australian National Curriculum and further evidence of ACSA's cultural-left bias can be found in its response to the review's final report. The way history is taught in schools is condemned as privileging 'a monolithic Anglo-centric/ Eurocentric view'. As such the argument is put the curriculum must embed in all subjects Aboriginal and Torres Strait Islander historical, spiritual and cultural perspectives.

ACSA also criticises the review's recommendation the curriculum 'better recognise the contribution of Western civilisation (and) our Judeo-Christian heritage' on the basis Australia is a multicultural, multifaith society and all cultures must be treated equally. Not unexpectedly ACSA concludes the review unfairly downplays the vital significance of teaching students about sustainability and climate change.

Conclusion

… by definition, there can be no education philosophy that does not address what learning is for. Confucius, Plato, Quintilian, Cicero, Comenius, Erasmus, Locke, Rousseau, Jefferson, Russell, Montessori, Whitehead and Dewey—each believed that there was some transcendent political, spiritual or social ideal that must be advanced through education.

Neil Postman. (1993).
Technopoly: The Surrender of Culture to Technology.

As argued by the American academic Neil Postman, education can never be value free as whatever position adopted concerning the work of schools and their relationship to society involves making judgements drawing on a particular philosophy or belief system.

For most of the 20th century a liberal view of education has dominated on the assumption all students need to become familiar with those subjects associated with what Oakeshott describes as a conversation, although drawing on a number of cultures, unique to Western civilisation and one that embraces continuity a well as change.

To be educated in its fullest sense is to experience subjects like mathematics, science, music, art, history, English, geography as well as sport and physical education. While evolving over time and being open to critique and re-evaluation core aspects of such subjects can be traced back to the early Greek and Roman philosophers and sophists and more recent events including the Enlightenment.

While often condemned as enforcing what the Italian Marxist Antonio Gramsci describes as cultural hegemony and thus treating students as passive victims of the capitalist system a liberal education rather than indoctrination and enforcing mindless group think is dedicated to fostering independent thought, rationality and critical awareness.

Poems by William Blake, Jonathan Swift' *Gulliver's Travels*, Machiavelli's *The Prince*, the plays of Bertolt Brecht and Arthur Miller and more recently Solzhenitsyn's *The Gulag Archipelago* are all literary works questioning and critiquing the status quo and championing the right to dissent and disagree.

Unlike an education based on neo-Marxist inspired critical theory that promotes a soulless, utilitarian and extreme secular agenda, a liberal education teaches the importance of the imagination and a spiritual and transcendent sense of life. As argued by William Blake, poetry provides a unique way of understanding the world by cleansing the doors of perception. He writes 'He who sees the Infinite in all things sees God. He who sees the Ratio only, sees himself only'.

A liberal education, drawing on Matthew Arnold's *Culture and Anarchy*, Cardinal Newman's *The Idea of a University* and the writings of the Catholic philosopher and theologian Saint Thomas Aquinas is also essentially moral in character as it embodies virtues such as justice, wisdom, moderation and courage as well as faith, hope and love.

As noted by Iain T. Benson from Australia's Notre Dame University, an education based on virtues is the opposite to one based on critical theory that is essentially political and utilitarian in nature directed at radically transforming society into its utopian image.

Involving a heady mix of neo-Marxism, feminism, postmodernism, deconstructionism and gender and postcolonial theories, what students encounter is superficial and lacking in moral substance and integrity. As a result, generations of students are leaving school culturally illiterate, morally adrift and programmed to be new-age warriors of the cultural-left.

Dr Kevin Donnelly AM is a Senior Research Fellow at the Australian Catholic University. He taught for 18 years as a secondary school teacher, was a member of the Panel of Examiners for Year 12 English and a member of the Victorian Board of Studies. In 2014 Kevin co-chaired the review of the Australian National Curriculum and in 2016 Kevin was made a Member of the Order of Australia in the Queen's birthday honour's list for services to education.

Since first warning about the dangers of political correctness during the early 1990s Kevin has established a reputation as one of Australia's leading conservative commentators and authors fighting against the cultural-left ideology that is poisoning society and stifling free and open debate. Political correctness denies the ability to reason and be impartial as knowledge is defined as a social construct and all relationships are based on privilege and power. In opposition, Kevin champions the strengths and benefits of Western civilisation, liberalism and our Judeo-Christian heritage that underpin our political and legal systems and that are being undermined by a rainbow alliance of neo-Marxist, postmodern theories. Kevin writes for the UK based The Conservative Woman and Sydney's Daily Telegraph and appears regularly on Sky News (kevindonnelly.com.au).

UNIVERSITIES

JENNIFER ORIEL

The free world stands on the shoulders of giants, but university leaders have so diminished freedom that the miseducated are leading the uneducated into a realm of darkness. The highest purpose of the university, to cultivate the flourishing of high culture and bequeath its bounty to future generations, is all but lost. Academics who benefitted from classical education watched universities transformed from sites of higher learning into revolutionary colleges during the late 1960s. Politics replaced the pursuit of truth, beauty and harmony as the raison d'être of higher education. Today, the university is a hollow man stripped of purpose and devoid of substance.

The most memorable part of a university should be its great scholars, but on modern university campuses, the best and brightest often comes from the past. As in many colonised countries, the most inspirational part of Australian campus life is the best of the British Empire. Yet the classical architecture, vaulted ceilings, whispering cloisters, sprawling lawns, deciduous trees, whimsical paintings and bronze busts are all a vision of history lost. They are dragged down for retrospective offences against state-designated minority groups, overshadowed by brutalist architecture, deconstructed and reconstructed to please the politically correct. And all the while, beauty is replaced by a simulation that is culturally impotent.

Cancel culture is a symbol of cultural impotence. It is the answer of the sterile mind to the flourishing of fertile thought. Those who cannot create, destroy. There is another way, but it requires humility to admit what you do not know and only those who suffer the reality check of an IQ test, or dedicate their spare time to reading great works know the limits of their intelligence. Without such learning, many people come to believe they are omniscient and feel a sense of entitlement to uproot culture. As such, they feel exhilaration instead of shame as they destroy what took centuries of genius to create: Western civilisation.

'Hey Hey Ho Ho, Western Civ has got to go.' In January 1987, black rights activist Jesse Jackson led 500 students in a protest against Stanford University. They resented a humanities department course that featured 15 masterpieces from the world's greatest living civilisation because of the authors' skin colour. The philosophers and literary masters were too fair by far and the activists wanted thinkers with darker skin on the curriculum. The demand for race-based curricular choices was issued by the black student organisation at Stanford. *The New York Times* documented a year later that feminists had joined the minority student cause to radicalise the curriculum. What followed was a wave of racist attacks on universities where the victims were usually people with white skin, but the main objective was the destruction of Western culture. It became known as the culture wars.

The influence of 1960's left activists in revolutionising higher education is astonishing in historical terms. A study of American public universities showed that in 1964, 82 per cent of public universities offered Western civilisation as a sequence. By 2010, it was 10 per cent.

The most popular book on the culture wars was published in the same year as the Stanford race protests. In *The Closing of the American Mind*, Allan Bloom argued that mass higher education did not demand the destruction of Western civilisation. Like many brilliant scholars, he did not anticipate popular appeal. But his book made the *New York Times* bestseller list and sold more than a million copies. What moved the reading public was more than Bloom's elegiac prose and searing conclusion that identity politics, pop culture and science without soul were debasing democracy. It was that the great betrayal of the free world was unfolding and campus activists – student, bureaucratic and academic – were destroying the soul of democracy by depriving youth of classical Western education.

The lesson of Bloom's book went beyond its redemptive quality. The unintended result of its publication was to reveal the deeply anti-democratic nature of the modern humanities. High profile academics such as Martha Nussbaum went low in questioning Bloom's intellectual abilities. A haggle of humanities academics poured scorn on him at an event co-sponsored by Duke University and the University of North Carolina. In the *New York Times*, Richard Bernstein wrote of the affair, later comparing it to the minute of hate in George Orwell's dystopian novel *1984*. The message was clear; the defence of Western civilisation was politically incorrect and those who promoted reason over revolution were the new dissident class.

If the academic world had taken more interest in Australia during the early 1980s, they might have seen the culture wars coming. The most famous purge in Australian university history occurred in 1984. Geoffrey Blainey was Dean of the Arts Faculty at the University of Melbourne. At the time, he was also chairman of the Australia-China Council and broadly recognised as the nation's foremost historian. None of that mattered when race activists came for him.

Blainey's political crime was to criticise the multicultural policy of the day on the grounds that government was introducing high levels of immigration from Asia at a time of widespread unemployment in Australia. Within months of the history professor discussing the matter of public interest at a public forum, students, socialist activists and academics went on the offensive. They protested his lectures on campus and off. Fellow history academics denounced him in a letter published in the provincial newspaper, *The Age*. Activists broke into the building where he was taking a history tutorial. Instead of defending their august professor, university management shut down his lectures, citing security grounds. Geoffrey Blainey, Australia's greatest living historian, was cancelled.

Cancel culture represents the consolidation of illiberal tendencies in Western universities, media and law. What began as political correctness in the 1960s has developed into a regime of thought control so oppressive that it is codified in law and higher education policy across the West.

For decades, Western writers have warned about the consequences of politicising higher education. By abandoning the classical approach to Western thought that is grounded in reason, disinterested scholarly inquiry and public debate, students would be left incapable of understanding the form of freedom and defending the culture of liberty for future generations.

The idea that universities exist to provide more than job training dates back to ancient Greece, the birthplace of the university. In the Greek concept of paideia, the purpose of advanced learning was to encourage the development of citizens capable of guarding high culture. The ideal inspired later Christian writers in the tradition of logos. As the late English philosopher Roger Scruton wrote in the journal *First Things*, moral education remained a part of university studies throughout the Middle Ages. The virtuoso ideal of the Renaissance inspired a new curriculum, the studia humaniores. In his essay, 'The End of the University', Scruton concluded there was little hope for the institution imagined by Cardinal Henry Newman in his famous 19th century book *The Idea of a University*. The aim of cultivating gentlemen would seem quaint today and high culture is held in low esteem.

In the place of the civilising campus has come the banal, brutalising education of the revolutionary college.

Freedom of speech is the canary in the mine that warns of totalitarianism seeping through the foundations of democracy. Increasingly serious cases of political censorship on campus are making headlines across the world. In recent years, Australians have borne witness to the protracted punishment of students who criticise race apartheid, the academic censure of protest against Chinese Communist Party influence in higher education, the prosecution of a well-respected professor who questioned climate science, as well the denouncement and cancellation of speakers poised to present politically incorrect views on race, climate change and transgender politics.

Several universities rejected a centre on Western civilisation even as they happily hosted academic centres dedicated to the study of Islamic culture and communist led Confucius Institutes. The Ramsay Centre was rejected because it stood poised to offer a study of the continuous history of Western civilisation rather than a politically correct curriculum that damns the West and deifies the rest.

Campus censorship is directed both at individuals, political groups and curriculum perceived as pro-Western or socially conservative. As such, the censorship is systemic and cultural. It will take cultural change measures to create a more politically diverse curriculum and professoriate.

University policies are so wanting of substantive protections for freedom that the National Tertiary Education Union argued for the inclusion of academic freedom in enterprise bargaining agreements. But only by incorporating in federal law the rights to freedom of speech and impartial scholarly inquiry can government compel university management to defend truth. Leading universities have rejected the notion of such legislation, but the Liberal Coalition government is proceeding with reform despite opposition.

While the censorship of reasoned argument on campus is greatly problematic, the selective nature of the silencing should be recognised as a form of discrimination. Yet it can be protected under discrimination law if it benefits a state-designated 'minority' group. For example, the University of Sydney Union guidelines for a debating championship included quotas for certain identity groups: 'At least four non-cis-male women-identifying people must be selected in the top three teams … one non-cis-male women-identifying person in each funded team'.

The university is a civilisation building enterprise. It reflects prevailing cultural norms and the beliefs of the ruling elite. In the Western world, the university exists to provide a culture of higher learning where academics teach the young how to explore great questions, argue well, discover truth, discard falsehood and become citizens capable of cultivating civil society. The most vital purpose of university is to teach people how to think. But in recent years, the university mission has been corrupted by thinkers of a lesser tradition who believe the purpose of education is to teach students what to think, not how to think.

As each generation passes through the ivory tower, the future of Western culture is extended as students grow into citizens who cultivate freedom of thought and speech as living articles of faith. The great betrayal of the West has been an academic war against liberty of thought and action that began, ironically, as a movement for liberation.

The origins of PC are disputed, but the master of the method was founder of the Chinese Communist Party and the world's most successful commander of genocide, Mao Zedong. Mao's mob targeted freethinkers deemed 'right-wing' who did not support the socialist revolution.

In his paper, 'On the Correct Handling of Contradictions Among the People', Mao explained that political correctness would be enforced by censoring dissent: 'What should our policy be towards non-Marxist ideas? As far as ... saboteurs of the socialist cause are concerned, the matter is easy, we simply deprive them of their freedom of speech' (Mao Zedong, 1957).

The CCP 'deprived' Chinese people who disagreed with militant left politics by imprisoning, torturing and killing them. Some were recruited by the communist party where they were trained in correct thought and commissioned to spy on other intellectuals the party wanted to purge. Other freethinkers were sent to revolutionary colleges established for the purpose of re-educating dissidents to accept Marxist ideology as truth.

Chinese President Xi Jinping has openly praised Maoism, saying: 'Dialectical materialism is the worldview and methodology of Chinese Communists ... the foundation is Marxist philosophy ... Mao cleverly applied the worldview and methodology of dialectical materialism, gave distinctive Chinese characteristics to Marxist philosophy, and set a shining example for our Party'.

To read Mao's works it to understand that he was a brilliant political strategist and an adept tactician with a deep understanding of human nature. He used it to create a politics devoid of moral goodness and the one party communist state that governs China with an iron fist. But he is unique among genocidal leaders of the 20th century for the degree to which he created enduring conformity by using a combination of social pressure and re-education. It is in Zedong's theory that we find the genesis of political correctness (PC) and its development into cancel culture where dissenters are publicly denounced, found guilty without trial and sentenced to a life in exile from the university, often losing their livelihoods in the process.

Students celebrate the silencing of dissent because they do not understand that as they win the power to censor, they lose ability to reason. It is human nature to be lazy and seek the easy way out. Silencing opposition is far easier than listening to an opponent and learning how to argue well. The act of destruction is cheap and exciting. The act of creation is exacting.

Although politics was never far from campus governance, after the 1960s and '70s, it became an academic affair. The aim of higher learning, the pursuit of objective truth and the classical liberal education in how to think were replaced by a revolutionary education that taught students what to think.

As communism maintained its grip on the East and the Islamic world fell under the spell of charismatic jihad, a new left politics was born in America. Its promise was equality. Its leaders were Marxist. Its spirit was militant, and its legacy is tyranny. What began as a movement for civil rights became a destructive force against both freedom and genuine equality on campus.

The New Left produced a radical transformation of the university from a place of higher learning to a site of political activism. The humanities was remade in the image of a new ideology called neo-Marxism.

While many activists contributed to the revolution, the principal architect of New Left thought was the brilliant theorist Herbert Marcuse. He is perhaps the most forgotten leader of the modern left. Students do not know that when they deplatform conservatives, demand that people who offend state-protected minorities are censored or think reflexively that the word minority means true disadvantage, they are doing the work of Marcuse.

In 1965, Marcuse justified a new form of inequality that would be made manifest by censoring right-of-centre freethinkers. In 'Repressive Tolerance', he wrote: 'The conclusion reached is that the realization of the objective of tolerance would call for intolerance toward prevailing policies, attitudes, opinions, and the extension of tolerance to policies, attitudes, and opinions which are outlawed or suppressed ... what is proclaimed and practiced as tolerance today, is in many of its most effective manifestations serving the cause of oppression'.

Marcuse was one of the Frankfurt School's most successful exports and worked in the long shadows of Italian communist Antonio Gramsci who sought to transform the West by a long march through the institutions. In his book *The Rotten Heart of Europe*, economist and EU critic Bernard Connolly revealed that one of the founding members of the Frankfurt School, Willi Munzenberg, proclaimed that the West must fall for communism to rise. He said it was necessary to 'organise the intellectuals and use them to make the Western civilisation stink. Only then, after they have corrupted all its values and made life impossible, can we impose dictatorship of the proletariat'.

Neo-Marxists began their revolution in universities and socialism led by a new proletariat class: radical minorities. Marcuse's equation for new Left equality demanded, 'Not equal, but more representation of the Left' (Marcuse, 1969, p. 133). The left moved away from the aim of civil rights, which was equal treatment under the law. Instead, it devised a system stacked against critics of the politically correct. It became known as affirmative action, or minority rights where members of the minority are not necessarily disadvantaged but usually reliable supporters of left-wing politics and politicians. Thus, women were included along with an ever-expanding list of identity groups.

Marcuse argued for a new form of inequality won by censoring dissent. He wrote that a 'subversive majority' could be established by 'undemocratic means' including 'the withdrawal of toleration of speech and assembly' from groups that dissented from left-wing politics. He proposed 'rigid restrictions on … educational institutions' and 'intolerance toward scientific research' that did not support his proposed revolutionary aims.

In respect of political correctness and what would become known as cancel culture, Marcuse seemed to channel Mao. He demanded 'intolerance … toward thought, opinion, and word … [of] conservatives [and] the political Right'. In the final score, he justified militancy and revolutionary violence by appeal to the Chinese communist revolution, among others. He dedicated his thesis of repressive tolerance to his students at Brandeis University.

Five decades later, his influence and legacy loomed large when students from Brandeis demanded that the university withdraw the offer of an honorary degree to freedom fighter Ayaan Hirsi Ali. Her thought crime was Islamophobia. According to former member of The International Institute for Islamic Thought, Abdur-Rahman Muhammad, Islamophobia is a 'loathsome term … nothing more than a thought-terminating cliche conceived in the bowels of Muslim think tanks for the purpose of beating down critics' (Abdur-Rahman cited in Horowitz & Spencer, *Islamophobia: Thought Crime of the Future*, 2011, pp. 14-15). Like so many before and since, Hirsi Ali was cancelled for being politically incorrect.

Unlike my liberal colleagues, I think the university should be a safe space; a place where students and staff can explore great ideas, ask unfashionable questions, engage in disinterested scholarly inquiry, state objective truth and disseminate knowledge without fear of penalty. However, research suggests that campus life is decidedly censorious. A study by the US-based Brookings Institute found that half of undergraduate students think it is acceptable to silence speech they find upsetting. Left-wing students were far more likely to support silencing speakers by shouting them down than students who leaned Republican (39 per cent and 62 per cent respectively.) The most shocking finding was that nearly one fifth of students (19 per cent) believed violence was an acceptable method of silencing dissenters.

As in the 1970s, race has been used as a weapon to justify

increasingly militant tactics on campus. But any self-declared minority will do, and, in the UK, the students are just as militant as their American comrades. In 2018, the Queer society at London's Goldsmiths University wanted to bring back the gulags for thought crime, describing them as 'a far cry from the Western, capitalist notion of prison. The aim was to correct and change the ways of "criminals"'.

Those who insist that defending truth is what matters in higher education pay a premium for moral courage, or even scientific rigour. Consider professor Peter Ridd, a highly respected scientist who managed the James Cook University marine geophysical laboratory for 15 years. His expertise includes the study of the Great Barrier Reef. There are few—if any—Australian academics better qualified to critique scientific research on the subject. However, after Ridd openly questioned the validity of university climate research he was dismissed. Management claimed he had breached a code of conduct about the university being a 'safe and respectful' workplace. Thankfully, university claims to autonomy have not placed them beyond the reach of democratic law. In 2019, Judge Salvatore Vasta found the university's dismissal of Ridd unlawful. In a blistering ruling, Vasta wrote: 'Incredibly, the university has not understood the whole concept of intellectual freedom', which he described as the core mission of institutions of higher learning. The university is appealing the ruling.

Several Australian universities regulate speech by providing language guidelines. Some were described in the Robert French review of freedom of speech in Australian universities. Curtin University in Western Australia provides Inclusive Language Procedures. Students and staff are to 'avoid stereotyping' on the basis of attributes used in discrimination law. However, the range of protected attributes goes beyond federal law to include 'national origin', 'family status' and 'gender history'.

At La Trobe University in Victoria, the Developing Inclusive Curriculum policy states that the curriculum should value the culture of all students, be responsive and give expression to the knowledge base of students and staff, and acknowledge that any curriculum decision is a selection rather than a complete truth. But it is reasonable to expect that if the culture professed by a student is backward, primitive, bigoted, given to violence, totalitarianism, or antipathy towards more advanced cultures, a scholar of the humanities would reject it in the interest of humanity. Surely the purpose of an academic is to be sufficiently well educated to discern what is worth defending on the curriculum. By contrast, the requirements of the inclusive curriculum sound like the consciousness-raising sessions popularised by cultural feminists in the 1970s.

Writing during the most violent period of the neo-Marxist colonisation of the university, sociologist Robert Nisbet lamented: 'I do not see how the university can conceivably fulfill the mission of detached scholarship, of objective study of ideas and values, within circumstances such as those prevailing at the present time … on the importance of depoliticization there can be no question'. But the university was not depoliticised. Instead, the revolutionary left marched through the cloisters leaving a trail of destruction in its wake.

The revolution began with scapegoating, isolating and purging classical and conservative thinkers from universities and then deepened into the curriculum where Western Civilisation was erased. The call for equality became totalitarian when revolutionaries pursued special privileges for minorities under affirmative action and discrimination legislation. Neo-Marxism replaced the Marxist ideal of a dictatorship of the proletariat with a dictatorship of the minoritariat.

The force required to defend regimes of codified inequality is great and over time, it breeds resentment in the excluded class. In the case of the West, the group excluded from the neo-Marxist minority politics enshrined in affirmative action law is the white, heterosexual, able-bodied male. And thus, the cry of student radicals as they deface the past is goodbye to dead white men.

Totalitarians share with the neo-Marxist radical minorities a hatred of Western Civilisation because the method of Western thought creates independence in the individual and freedom in society. Mao identified what we would call classical liberal philosophy as a principal threat for that reason. Communists targeted freethinkers schooled in classical liberal thought because they were not vulnerable to the emotional appeals used to indoctrinate the 'uncritical masses'. As a result, they were more likely to question the validity of socialist theory. As a consequence, Mao turned his attention to the re-education of liberal-minded citizens. From 1948-1952, his 'revolutionary colleges' were established across China to introduce communist ideology as national culture.

Marcuse acknowledged that the New Left student movement, which regarded him as a godhead, was influenced by Maoism. The effects of the New Left revolution across university campuses bear all the hallmarks of Mao's cultural revolution. In the thirty-five years following the anti-conservative censorship regime prescribed in 'Repressive Tolerance', affirmative action and censorship of speech deemed offensive to radical minorities has become standard policy across Western universities.

The sustained attack on the fundamental Western values of freedom of thought, speech and public reason is an obstacle to human progress. A civilisation advances as citizens are set free to explore great questions and test certainties in science, medicine and the humanities. When the truth is not set free, human progress grinds to a halt. It is part of the reason why totalitarian regimes fail to produce creative genius and perform better at tweaking the inventions they so often steal from free world countries.

The battle for the free world rages as liberal democracies are in decline and totalitarian powers are on the ascendancy in Asia and the Middle East. The money from foreign students, especially Chinese nationals, influences how university administrators approach the question of freedom. Their reputation is their brand power and universities are big business. But it is not enough to beg the authority of money when the future of freedom is at risk.

University management has a moral duty to remember that in Nazi Germany and communist China, the university was transformed from a place of reason to a re-education camp. Truth was exiled as freethinkers fled to the West. If the Western university falls to the lesser gods of political correctness, there will be no refuge for freethinkers and no place for the spirit of freedom. The responsibility to save the ivory tower from modern day jackboots is not regional. It is global.

Jennifer Oriel is a weekly columnist for The Australian. *She has a PhD in political science from the University of Melbourne. She began as a higher education columnist before becoming a weekly political columnist. She has been cited in several books and the Australian Parliament for her analysis of Western civilisation, Islamic terrorism as a Western condition, and her critique of political correctness in education, medicine and the law. Her academic research has been featured on the syllabi of Harvard University, the University of London, the University of Toronto, Amherst College, the University of Wisconsin and Columbia University.*

FROM EDUCATION TO ENSTUPIDATION— TEACHING ENGLISH LANGUAGE AND LITERATURE IN AUSTRALIA

FIONA MUELLER

It is the duty of the State to educate, and the right of the people to demand education.
Edmund Barton, Prime Minister of Australia 1901-1903

There could well be grounds for a class action on behalf of young Australians let down by those who hold legislative responsibility for education.

With over 25 per cent of Year 7 students and one in five school leavers unable to achieve the national minimum standards in literacy, a team of investigative lawyers could make a strong case for policy failure and associated litigation.

Teachers who pay for university qualifications that do not reflect high levels of confidence and competence in the English language would likely put their students first by supporting such a case.

Exhibit A should be a forensic analysis of the decades of 'progressive' experiments in education that have left generations of Australians linguistically and intellectually impoverished. The nation has paid a high price for 'whole language', constructivist and inquiry-based approaches to learning, postmodernist literary theory, and writing instruction based on text types (genre theory), being just a few examples of the anti-intellectual and duplicitous movements that found their way into schooling during the last century.

In the new millennium, poorly designed curriculum documents that prioritise globalist agendas not only set low literacy expectations but also fail to give every young learner a deep appreciation of the unique literary tradition of the Western, English-speaking world, especially in terms of establishing one of the world's great liberal democracies and most open societies.

The Australian Curriculum, intended to set the expectations for learning across all states and territories, is an incohesive publication that has required years of investment in professional development for teachers (even though it was allegedly written for them) and constant (re)interpretation for other stakeholders. It neither inspires nor unites.

The failure to ground students in a strong sense of national identity, purpose and expectations should now add a critical dimension to any debate about the education of young Australians. Without such a framework, emphasising the distinctive and unifying characteristics of Australia's heritage, the nation's youngest citizens have no common, powerful intellectual anchors to hold on to at a time of crisis.

This chapter is dedicated to those who, as 2019 Thawley Essay Prize Winner Emma McCaul wrote in 'As history fades into history', 'know that something isn't right'.

But, as McCaul explains:

… we don't want to be the adults in the room and address the cause of our unease. Being useful idiots isn't what we want, but we have been betrayed and our ignorance of so much of what should be our heritage and legacy leaves us unable to make constructive criticism, or to give thanks.

This chapter is also for those who carry the torch for English language and literature, including parents, teachers and academics who contributed their thoughts. Many are aghast at the loss of respect for accurate, high-quality usage. They cite the price individuals pay for bucking the new fixation on political correctisms, victimhood and exclusive identity lenses that are, to borrow from the American political philosopher Allan Bloom, closing the Australian mind.

McCaul nails the great irony that 'Indigenous Australians know that history and culture must be fought for and proudly expressed if it is to be preserved and passed on to their children, but other Australians seem to have lost the will to take this path'.

In contrast, students in one of the world's most successful education systems are guided by a curriculum that aims to produce 'Concerned citizens who are rooted to Singapore, have a strong civic consciousness, are responsible to their family, community and nation and take active roles in improving the lives of others'.

In Singapore—where the language of instruction in schools is English and all students must learn at least one other language throughout their education—the curriculum stipulates that students 'Understand that national identity involves knowing the Singapore heritage and culture and how it has influenced our unique way of life, is important because it gives one a sense of belonging [and] shapes the Singaporean culture'.

This chapter is being written in the time of COVID-19. Around the world, leaders have forced children and their families into 'remote learning' for long periods, often with devastating implications for academic progress and mental wellbeing.

Students with low levels of confidence and competence in language—particularly reading and writing—and those who cannot rely on excellent curriculum and teaching are much more likely to suffer long term disadvantage. From 2021, the many deep and longstanding deficits in Australian education systems will make effective remediation very difficult.

In particular—considering that English is the only compulsory subject in Kindergarten to Year 12—there are enormous implications for teacher training. If the school curriculum lacks rigour and university undergraduate programs continue to follow politically correct guidelines, there is no hope for improvement in student performance.

Language and the left's long march

As with dodgy doctors preying on vulnerable people, the 'quackademics' in education use politically correct jargon to baffle and persuade. If the cisheteropatriarchy—that age-old system of power whereby straight, white men exploit and oppress women and the LGBTIQ+—could be eliminated, the world would be so much better off. Perfectly in line with George Orwell's portrayal of linguistic totalitarianism, the international 'quackademy' of activist academics is transforming English. This means new parameters for any speaker or author, and it includes cancelling and de-platforming speakers such as psychologist Jordan Peterson for rejecting government-mandated use of non-English personal pronouns or novelist Lionel Shriver for alleged cultural appropriation in her portrayal of African-American and Latino characters.

This transformation of the English language is not a thoughtful, shared movement designed to enhance communication and help future generations to build a stronger society.

The education 'quackademy' does its best to convince young learners that white privilege and androcentrism continue to repress people through racism, classism, capitalism, ableism, homophobia, xenophobia and all the other evils of the dominant culture.

Ideological and linguistic walls are now being built either to silence students or to send them out to the intellectual battlefield as desperately ignorant 'useful idiots' who have no idea how little they know.

The Marxists want a total reorientation of society and that means redefining and often eliminating traditional concepts—particularly around individual and national identity—as these have been established over centuries through English language and literature.

In some Californian schools, ethnic studies programs have worked in startlingly Orwellian ways since the 1970s to rework the English language in the name of helping teachers and students to make alternative words part of mainstream usage.

Apparently, all 'so-shul construkts' such as traditional spelling conventions stand in the way of a more equal world. What matters now is that culturally dominant words such as 'history' be changed to 'hxstory' as part of global social transformation. Being more inclusive, for example, can apparently be achieved by imposing gender-neutral pronouns such as 'ze' or 'hir', and making sure that people state their individual pronoun preferences when introducing themselves.

It is all very well to say that English—like the climate—is always changing, but there are critical consequences for those whose learning is so dependent upon the adults around them.

Australian higher education institutions produce tomorrow's teachers, but if intellectual rigour and a sound knowledge of language and literature are to remain academic goals, the future does not look too bright.

On condition of anonymity, one Australian university lecturer summarised the current situation, saying that 'It is now a commonplace in discussions of English literature at universities to say and to think that, as part of a larger European tradition, British English literary tradition is racist, sexist, misogynist, ethnocentric, imperialist, and homophobic'.

The lecturer further observes that, in his department, the coverage of Old English and Middle English (460-1100) is almost gone and studying major periods of English literature up to the 19th century is sparse.

What has taken its place? Courses in postcolonial literatures, Australian literature, women's writing, creative writing, and literary theory ... a student majoring in English literature in this department would have a very limited knowledge of the history of British literature in English, and the English language.

One English literature specialist says that those who teach works from the traditional canon of English literature (Caedmon's Hymn, Chaucer, Shakespeare, Milton, etc.) 'are often suspected and accused of being complicit in some way with the moral depravity at the heart of western society'.

Another lecturer believes that 'The idea that university campuses are places of free speech and robust debate is a joke'.

Students of all ages are now primed to look for academic transgressions, ready and able to attack any teacher whose approach does not fit the new cultural-left, politically correct literary standards.

A firsthand recount of the effects of cancel culture on one academic follows:

... after taking one of my third-year courses for which I assigned major canonical works of British and American English literature, a student wrote a letter to the Dean of Arts complaining that I failed to acknowledge and address the 'toxicity [that] pervades our every institution', I failed to 'recalibrate the inequality paradigm', and I failed to abide by the terms of the university's Equity and Diversity Policy. Represented as an uncritical member of institutions who perpetuated this toxicity and inequality and read literature through the lens of 'masculine ego', I felt defamed. I felt that, in order to keep my job and maintain my reputation, I had to be very guarded.

Spencer Klavan, the gifted Yale and Oxford graduate who hosts the podcast The Young Heretics, remembers the effects of academic narrowing on his own education: 'for certain teachers, you knew that only a certain range of views would fly. How well or poorly those views were defended mattered little or not at all: what mattered was which ones you held'. It is hypocrisy at a very deep level, he says, and 'the intriguing irony is that those teachers were also always the ones who stressed "critical thinking"—some of them even had a reputation for being free-thinking mavericks'.

According to Klavan, who identifies C.S. Lewis as 'the greatest intellectual of the 20th century', there is a 'golden thread that links Plato's Republic to Aristotle's Politics, running on down through the history of Western political and moral thought even to the present benighted day'.

English in Australia

This golden thread described by Klavan is no longer obvious in Australian school education. In New South Wales, once widely respected for setting the 'gold standard' in education, the curriculum simply acknowledges English as the national language and the only mandatory subject from Kindergarten to Year 12:

Developing proficiency in English enables students to take their place as confident communicators, critical and imaginative thinkers, lifelong learners and informed, active participants in Australian society. It supports the development and expression of a system of personal values, based on students' understanding of moral and ethical matters, and gives expression to their hopes and ideals.

Supporting the development of 'a system of personal values' without methodical reference to the great thinkers who have debated 'moral and ethical matters' for millennia, and who have influenced the evolution of free and open societies around the world, is inconceivable.

Senior secondary students (Years 11 and 12) study English literature to 'deepen their understanding of how texts represent individual and collective human experiences' and 'explore how texts may give insight into the anomalies, paradoxes and inconsistencies in human behaviour and motivations, inviting the responder to see the world differently, to challenge assumptions, ignite new ideas or reflect personally'. Although the Stage 6 syllabus makes brief mention of 'universal themes', and Shakespeare and some other writers with canonical status are prescribed for study across these courses, no clear case is made for the selection of texts as a means of educating students in, as Klavan puts it, 'the history of Western political and moral thought'.

At a national level, the Australian Curriculum could hardly be more utilitarian or less uplifting, particularly in relation to English language and literature. Where many might search for a sophisticated representation of the linguistic and literary foundations of Australia— smoothly integrated with the sciences and humanities as well as Civics and Citizenship and other relevant areas—the curriculum instead offers excruciatingly repetitive, long and boring lists about the mechanics of written expression and generic statements about the skills students are to acquire. Apart from encouraging a bureaucratic mentality that overwhelms teachers and reduces the subject to a box-

ticking exercise, there is little to stimulate the next generation of
Australian thinkers and writers.

Given his own preparation for the highest leadership position, what
would Edmund Barton say? Australia's first Prime Minister was a
prize-winning graduate in classics from the University of Sydney who
honed his speaking skills at the Sydney Mechanics' School of Arts.

Perhaps he would not mind that few 21st century students would
be able to identify him or describe his nation-building achievements,
but he might need convincing that current curriculum expectations
and the associated pedagogy as per the 2019 Alice Springs (Mparntwe)
Declaration 'truly promote the intellectual, physical, social, emotional,
moral, spiritual and aesthetic development and wellbeing of young
Australians' who are consequently well placed to ensure 'the nation's
ongoing economic prosperity and social cohesion'.

We cannot know the extent to which Barton was inspired by
particular authors, but close study of England's greatest playwright may
well have encouraged him, as in Shakespeare's King John, to:

Be great in act, as you have been in thought …
Grow great by your example,
and put on the dauntless spirit of resolution.

And what a great act of political midwifery he carried out. Sydney-
born and a passionate advocate of Federation, Barton was deservedly
proud to announce that 'For the first time in history, we have a nation
for a continent and a continent for a nation'.

As a barrister and aspiring politician, he backed the 1880 Public
Instruction Act in New South Wales which revolutionised access to
learning for all children aged between 6 and 14. Himself the youngest
of nine, whose well-educated mother ran a school for girls in the 1860s,
Barton supported the provision of free, compulsory education and
believed that schooling should be 'unsectarian'.

Based on decades of national and international test results (including
PIRLS, TIMSS and PISA where too many Australians miss the
benchmarks), official reports and public commentary, Barton might
well conclude that this country's youngest citizens are not thriving

academically in the 21st century.

Certainly, he would struggle to find evidence of improvements resulting from the billions of dollars allocated under the Gonski funding model and would be further disillusioned when reading the 2018 *Review to Achieve Educational Excellence in Australian Schools* and previous decades of ineffective reviews and reports.

Australia's first Prime Minister would search in vain for evidence that his beloved Greek and Latin still play a key role in the formation of younger generations, realising that today's curricula put minimal emphasis on appreciating the ancient foundations of the freedoms and opportunities they enjoy as citizens of one of the world's great democracies.

Barton, the scholarly lawyer and politician, would be bemused, if not scandalised, by the abysmally low national minimum standards set for the English language in the 21st century (Year 9 NAPLAN, for example), together with the lack of systematic exposure to millennia of great literature that would truly help to develop what the Australian Curriculum refers to as 'successful learners, confident and creative individuals, and active and informed citizens'.

The Prime Minister's speeches, delivered to city and country audiences from his buggy and in hundreds of unglamorous venues, are not remembered with the same reverence as Henry Parkes' 1889 Tenterfield Oration (an optional component of the Australian Curriculum's Humanities and Social Sciences for Years 5 and 6).

Nevertheless, that disciplined debater spoke so often and so persuasively about the Australian Federation that he set an undeniable example to young and old about the power of language to persuade and to inspire.

He would be relieved to see that a subsequent Prime Minister, Sir Robert Menzies—educated in a small regional town—mastered the English language so beautifully that he became one of Australia's greatest political orators (although Menzies does not appear on the Australian Curriculum's list of suggested texts for English).

However, Barton would find it difficult to identify any nationally consistent commitment to teaching intelligent, articulate debate. Once regarded as a key skill that helped to demonstrate wide knowledge, linguistic dexterity, oratory and the ability to think logically and rationally, debating is now almost despised by those who see it as an elitist practice from another age. Most Australian students do some oral presentations but even those are under threat because of the increase in performance anxiety and frequent requests to do these tasks with only the teacher as the audience.

Cancel culture and the death of civility and reason

One can only imagine Barton's reaction to the language of one of Australia's prominent advocates of public education, Jane Caro, who did not like the result of the May 2019 federal election:

Well, Australia may be f..ked and the whole planet not far behind but I am at the best, most brilliant and cool wedding I have ever been too (sic). So I shall just dance & get pissed & stick two rude fingers up to the truculent turds who voted to turn backwards.

Crude, abusive application of the English language and the refusal to engage in the intelligent exchange of ideas are antithetical to the 'deep knowledge' and 'critical thinking skills' that are hot topics for contemporary education policymakers.

Yet the cancellers have no sense of their own hypocrisy.

According to a *Sydney Morning Herald* article in 2015, 'The irrepressible Jane Caro has built a career out of words'. In 2018, the Melbourne University Press promotion of her book *Accidental Feminists* claimed that 'The common thread running through her career is a delight in words and a talent for using them to connect with other people'.

Connecting with other people clearly does not always include intellectual pluralism and tolerance, given that the cancellers' own words prove they have no respect for that universal human right, freedom of expression.

For centuries, children have been taught the Golden Rule of treating others as they would themselves like to be treated, both in word and in deed. With origins in Greek philosophy, and found in Matthew 7:12 of the New Testament, this is a principle shared by Buddhists, Jews, Confucians and others, encouraging human beings to work together for the common good.

That concept is the opposite of ideological intimidation—epitomised by cancel culture—that denies the right of others to hold varying political and philosophical positions. It is led by those who either do not value or have never studied the work of thinkers such as John Stuart Mill, for example, who explained so clearly that 'all silencing of discussion is an assumption of infallibility'.

Those lessons from the great writers have been lost to generations of young Australians.

But they are timelessly wise about the human condition. In pleading that Shylock spare Antonio's life, for example, Shakespeare's Portia appeals to the humanitarian instincts that should resonate with the 21st century global education agenda.

The quality of mercy is not strain'd
It droppeth as the gentle rain from heaven
Upon the place beneath: it is twice blest;
It blesseth him that gives and him that takes ...

And few Australian students will ever learn about how little mercy was shown to Oscar Wilde, the superbly witty, gay, Irish, Victorian-era writer of *The Picture of Dorian Gray, The Importance of Being Earnest* and *De Profundis*, among many other works. Through his lead female character in *Lady Windermere's Fan*, Wilde speaks to his audience about London society:

Actions are the first tragedy in life, words are the second. Words are perhaps the worst. Words are merciless...

One of Australia's most erudite citizens frequently reflects on what is happening to language and debate in the public square. Possibly channelling her former military role, Catherine McGregor has said that those who cannot tolerate dissenting worldviews simply deploy 'rhetorical stun grenades', shutting down unwanted exchanges with accusations of racism, sexism and transphobia, or by launching any other claim that can easily and artlessly be weaponised.

But today's young learners are not armed with the intellectual and linguistic knowledge and skills—particularly logic—that allow them to stand tall against the silencers.

They are not taught to debate, only to accuse.

Academic cancel culture motivated the Manhattan Institute's Heather MacDonald to write *The Diversity Delusion*. She believes that one of the greatest academic experiences any individual should have at university is 'to learn, to encounter works of extraordinary beauty, grandeur, wisdom, profundity ... four years to open your mind to what human beings have accomplished, what they overcame ...'.

But, says MacDonald, 'the poisonous politics of identity have taken over ... [it is] the encouragement of victimology ... the extreme constriction of what students think they want to learn and ought to learn. That thinking that the colour of one's skin or one's gender is the most important qualification is now transforming the world'.

Classic expectations

But how can students know what they should learn?

The 21st century education agenda reflects the one-world mantra of open borders and OECD proposals for 'the future we want', a key outcome being generic curriculum that could be implemented anywhere with a few tweaks. In Australia, the globalists and quackademics now advocate unsubstantiated approaches to teaching and learning that have no grounding in national identity, intellectual rigor, and a strong moral and ethical sense of character based on disciplined, wide reading.

Back in 1980s America, professor of education and humanities E. D. Hirsch wrote about generations of students being let down because of the failure to give every child access to shared, core knowledge that would make them culturally literate. He took the position that letting a child unfold naturally according to its own time clock like a ball of yarn is quite an unnatural proceeding for human beings. What is natural for a child is to be inducted into the particular language and value-orientations of a particular culture.

Faced with curricula and lists of suggested texts that are silent about the intellectual and linguistic heritage of their own country, young Australians have no sound basis on which to decide what to learn. Worse, they have no way of understanding the basis for decisions about what constitutes ethical behaviour and a commitment to the common good.

The New South Wales English curriculum mandates that 'the selection of texts must give students experience of texts which are widely regarded as quality literature'. Now there is a blank cheque.

Additionally, 'in selecting specific texts for study in English, teachers should consider the needs, interests and abilities of their students and the ethos of the school and its local community'.

Rather than leaving it to teachers to select texts that are 'widely regarded as quality literature', a better approach would be that of Spencer Klavan, who suggests looking to writers who simultaneously engage the heart, the mind and the soul. That expectation sets a far higher bar.

It is also key to improving Australian education, especially in an era when policymakers prefer to use vacuous buzzwords such as 'student engagement' and 'student agency', whereby young learners are somehow supposed to acquire '21st century competencies' that will make them into 'lifelong learners' and 'global citizens'.

Such fundamental contradictions help to explain the extremely short and seemingly random list of recommended 'classic texts' in the New South Wales English syllabus for Years 7–10 (although the list of suggested poems for older students is more comprehensive). One C.S. Lewis book, *The Lion, The Witch and The Wardrobe*, is part of a collection introduced by the statement that 'students will still continue to benefit from exposure to classics'.

There is a further clarification: 'Many of these texts can be made relevant to contemporary concerns. For instance, the aspects of racism raised in *To Kill a Mockingbird* are still as urgent as when the book was written'.

So students should read books that overtly address the -isms, but anyone looking for a more profound justification of the place of 'classic texts' within the literary tradition of the English-speaking world will be disappointed.

According to the authorities, 'the literary merit of the work and the needs, interests and abilities of readers have been balanced with the sensitivities of young and young adult readers. The texts on these lists were selected based on their potential to engage the reader using a number of strategies such as interesting characters, unusual settings and plots, and humour'. There is no hint of the golden thread of Australia's literary heritage.

Instead, the NSW K–10 syllabus says that texts must meet criteria such as:

Cultural, social and gender perspectives, Insights into Aboriginal experiences in Australia, Aspects of environmental and social sustainability, Intercultural experiences and Insights about the people and cultures of Asia, and texts from other countries and times.

This is the same syllabus that tells teachers that 'The brevity of some of the classic short stories makes them particularly accessible to students and includes the short stories of Anton Chekhov, Guy de Maupassant, W Somerset Maugham, O Henry, Edgar Allan Poe, Katherine Mansfield and Ray Bradbury'. In this official curriculum document, it seems, the rationale for choosing many classic texts is that they are short, or 'accessible'.

Turning soft heads around

The cancel culture threat to humanity's most extraordinary distinguishing feature—language—is playing out in English-speaking countries in ways that may prevent any improvements to the learning of young Australians.

Heather MacDonald laments that in America she sees:
both the opportunity cost of lost knowledge and their effect on society at large of introducing racial division, ethnic tension, gender anger … in

*a society that is in fact the most open and opportunity-filled in human
history.*

As Allan Bloom concluded over thirty years ago, 'lack of education
simply results in students' seeking for enlightenment wherever it is
readily available, without being able to distinguish between the sublime
and trash, insight and propaganda'.

And before him, C. S. Lewis worried about the teaching of English
when critiquing a 1939 textbook titled *The Control of Language: A
Critical Approach to Reading and Writing.* In his beautifully concise
feedback to the authors (who happened to be Australians Alec King and
Martin Ketley), Lewis argues in *The Abolition of Man* that 'By starving
the sensibility of our pupils we only make them easier prey to the
propagandist when he comes. For famished nature will be avenged and
a hard heart is no infallible protection against a soft head'.

In 1989 Bloom saw the literary future, saying that 'Teachers of
writing in state universities, among the noblest and most despised
laborers in the academy, have told me that they cannot teach writing
to students who do not read, and that it is practically impossible to get
them to read, let alone like it'.

One Australian high school English teacher says that the
expectations are 'bare minimum'.

*It's ridiculous that in some Year 11 and 12 courses students are only
required to read the opening page or one chapter or one poem from lots
of different authors. This is supposed to enable them to compare styles
so that they can develop a distinctive style and be inspired to create their
own work. So they can spend a whole term just reading extracts, even
from the greatest works such as Homer's* Odyssey.

Another view is that 'Australia gets this really wrong. They call them
English courses but they don't take a holistic approach that ensures that
students leave school with a good command of the English language as
well as an exposure to really great writing'.

Nineteenth century writer Jane Austen, whose work still gets
attention in some schools, wrote in *Northanger Abbey* that 'The person,
be it gentleman or lady, who has not pleasure in a good novel, must be

intolerably stupid'. A cynic would add that since Austen is female, she instantly gets a tick for diversity and can thus get away with criticising unenthusiastic readers.

Once upon a time, a high-quality education in Australia included sustained study of at least one ancient or modern language, but it is to this multicultural country's shame that so few students can take advantage of high-quality programs.

Not only would better provision soon lift results in English literacy, it would be proof of a genuine commitment to the national aims to 'equip young Australians with the skills, knowledge and understanding that will enable them to engage effectively with and prosper in a globalised world ... [to] gain personal and social benefits, be better equipped to make sense of the world in which they live and make an important contribution to building the social, intellectual and creative capital of our nation'.

It would also show that policymakers and educators are genuinely interested in the evidence of what works. The benefits for students' literacy skills and cognitive development are documented in decades of research and are in evidence every day in high-performing education systems.

As Finnish researcher Irina Buchberger has explained, 'this has been a reality in the Finnish education system since the early seventies— multilingual Finnish citizens competent in four languages [including English]'. In Finland, language competence is 'a key element in the personal and professional development of individuals'.

Rather than leaping on the latest politically correct bandwagon, Australian policymakers should be using the best available evidence to improve teaching and learning.

Taxpayers should get their money back and students and teachers should be paid compensation for the great English language and literature swindle that so often fails to 'create confident communicators, imaginative thinkers and informed citizens'.

Dr Fiona Mueller has a comprehensive teaching, leadership and policy background in schools, universities and government bodies. Fiona co-authored a policy paper on school education for the Page Research Centre, with a particular emphasis on nation-building, academic standards and access for rural, regional and remote students. Originally a teacher of foreign languages and head of department in secondary schools, Fiona joined the former NSW Board of Studies (now NESA) to develop new HSC curricula in 2000, going on to complete a doctorate and teach at two universities. She became Head of ANU College at the Australian National University in 2014 and then took on a national role as Director of Curriculum at the Australian Curriculum, Assessment and Reporting Authority (ACARA), collaborating with education authorities across all sectors and participating in multiple international research projects. Her experience with students and their families in a range of educational settings enables her to approach policy development with a deep understanding of the opportunities and challenges of Kindergarten to Year 12 and post-school pathways. She is an Adjunct Scholar with the Sydney-based Centre for Independent Studies.

THE RADICALISING OF HISTORY AND WHAT TO DO ABOUT IT

DAVID DAINTREE

From time to time a brief chance encounter leads to long reflection. Two or three decades ago I found myself in a tiny township in South-West Queensland. The only building of substance there was a quaint little courthouse, over a hundred years old, modestly furnished for the most part, but dominated by a fine polychrome version of the Royal Arms above the judgement seat. It made a huge impression on me and I asked myself—and asked many students in later years—why was it there?

The easy answer was that it is a remnant of British colonial rule, which is true as far as it goes, but there's much more to it than that. To begin to understand it fully one has to go back as far as the reign of Henry II, King of England 1154–1189, whose ardour for the equitable administration of justice led to the development of regional courts and assizes as well as the expansion of the jury system to enable his subjects throughout the land to receive the King's justice without having to attend the King's principal Court in person.

Only against that backdrop can one grasp the full story of that little Queensland courthouse (and thousands like it throughout the world) that dispensed justice to all in the King's name. Culture war activists argue that the arrival of the First Fleet led to genocide and the destruction of the Aboriginal culture. The counter argument is that it represents the arrival of liberal ideas and the British Common Law. One of the books that came with the convict settlement was Blackstone's Commentaries on the Laws of England, with its noble assertion that slavery is repugnant to reason, and that 'a slave or negro, the instant he lands in England, becomes a free man'.

Of course even with Henry II the story is incomplete, for the whole story about anything is always beyond the full comprehension of ordinary human individuals. But Henry II and his policies amount to a very important element of the story that ought to be known by anybody with a serious interest in understanding Australian History. There's an even bigger picture lurking in the background: the close links between Christianity and the Common Law go back to the conversion of the Anglo-Saxon nations in England yet have been largely pushed into the background by a thoroughly secularised legal system whose practitioners now seem to take less interest in jurisprudence than in matters of financial compensation for injuries, real or purported.

Roman Law, too, though pagan in origin, was transformed in the Institutes of Justinian and other jurists of the late Empire into a deeply Christian body of legal doctrine. Even the best legal system is a somewhat blunt instrument in its handling of complex moral questions in which the conscience and the intentions of individuals are at issue, but Roman Law like Common Law recognised the sovereignty of God as the source of all true justice.

So why are so many history students unaware of, or what is worse indifferent to, the historical context and the legal and cultural background of the phenomena they seek to understand? And why do so many academics committed to post-colonial theory argue that there is nothing beneficial or worthwhile in Western Civilisation, as if countries like Australia are riven with structural racism and white supremacism? To try to answer that question, I should like to consider three more cases in which the glib and easy answer seems to satisfy the curiosity of most students who engage in the study of History.

Let us begin with the First World War. What caused it? Certainly the assassination of an archduke in Sarajevo sparked the conflict and was the immediate trigger, but the whole picture is as always far more complicated than that. Residual bitterness on both sides following the largely pointless fiasco of the Franco-Prussian War was a contributing factor, as was the greedy competition among many of the European nations for colonial possessions in Africa. The uneasy partnership of Britain and her old ally France, as well as Russia in the east, challenged and provoked the awakening nationalism of imperial Germany as she united under the hegemony of Prussia.

The second case is that of slavery, always an extraordinarily complex and emotive issue, particularly now as the Black Lives Matter movement stalks our public life, pulling down statues and re-writing history. Current thinking understandably casts Europeans in the role of arch villains in that despicable trade. I say understandably because the European slave trade is better documented, or at least better known, than any other. And indeed the cruelty and greed of traffickers from Western nations cannot be ignored or condoned. We know that European traders purchased slaves in exchange for raw materials such as iron, textiles and gold. All that is true. But from whom did they purchase them?

The awful truth is that Africans sold Africans, and that Arab slave traders were also active in the trade, not only in Africa but in the Mediterranean as well. It has been calculated that 12 million Africans were sold to Western nations and transported to the New World. The number of slaves sold to other African and Arab peoples will probably never be known but is certainly greater. If we seriously want to find heroes in the eradication of Western slavery our first discovery will be Great Britain and the Royal Navy. From 1833 onwards British sailors fought against slavery not only within their own Empire but throughout the world. It is seriously counter-cultural and no doubt seen as inflammatory to say so, but it was white men who finally abolished slavery in the Western world. William Wilberforce and so many other courageous and inspirational Christians led the movement.

Yet despite the high cost in lives and sacrifice born by those who sailed the malaria-infested coasts of Africa, slavery within Africa and the Middle East, undertaken in Muslim countries and largely airbrushed from history, seems to have survived little impaired. This, of course, is popular history embarrassingly turned on its head. Slavery is a far more difficult issue to deal with than any war. The appalling sufferings of soldiers in the First World War can never be forgotten, though in the initial stages at least this was a combat between volunteers. Yes, jingoistic attitudes on both sides drove men to the recruiting stations, and combatants were able to hope for an eventual end to hostilities, if not in time for Christmas.

I do not make light of the awfulness of what ensued for them after the early patriotic exuberance wore itself out. But for slaves there is no hope, no respite. Their lives were so cheap that traders could accept high death rates on the dreaded Middle Passage as the price of carrying capacity cargoes. A captured slave ship might drown its entire cargo (the poor souls chained together at the neck) to avoid capture and prosecution after the trade became illegal. It was all utterly and unrelievedly monstrous.

History has an important role to play here. Ignorance may be both bliss and comfort. If we can persuade ourselves (it's not hard to do) that all slavers were white European males we effortlessly impose our own form of racism on the world, passing all the blame to white men, and of course to their descendants. So if we pull down the statues of anybody who had a connection with slavery, the world is put to rights.

It's not that simple. The records show that slavery has been practised almost universally in human societies of all races and on all continents, other than Antarctica. In Australia, the charge of slavery has been levelled at both the import of indentured labourers, such as the Kanakas, and at the practice of child marriage among some Aboriginal communities, but neither instance can be shown to meet the minimum standards of definition. Most importantly, it rarely seems to have been true that members of one major racial group confined their activities to enslaving members of another: Greeks enslaved Greeks, Celts enslaved Celts, Africans enslaved Africans, and piratical Arab traders enslaved anybody they could lay their hands on. It is an easy and convenient cop-out to blame it all on Europeans and to confine all our sympathy to black slaves. Paradoxically the classification of all Africans as one amorphous people is radically racist, for it neglects the important differences between ethnic groups.

Are we speaking of Somali, Hausa, Shona or Zulu? To ignore this is as shallow—and as pointless—as grouping all Europeans together as if they amount to one cultural group, or all Asians as if they shared common origins and outlooks. Historically slavery has been an almost universal practice and one extremely difficult to eradicate. In the matter of slavery, what nation, black, white or brindle, has clean hands? Horrifyingly, UN agencies estimate that there are still 40 million slaves in the world today, three times as many as were transported from Africa to the New World in the infamous Middle Passage.

My third case is the Crusades. This prolonged series of military exercises, backed by the spiritual authority of the Church, is a continuing source of embarrassment and shame to many people in the West. They are the perfect expression, so the prevailing narrative goes, of the unpleasantly warlike tendencies of White Christians, who invaded the territories of peace-loving Muslims without provocation, and did so with ruthless cruelty. That is the widely accepted picture. Muslims committed to the 'de-colonisation' of the curriculum of course see little problem with that interpretation of events, and so far as I am aware show no sign of being stricken by pangs of conscience over their extensive conquests.

But should we who are heirs of the Western Christian tradition be so gullible as to accept all the guilt without examination, and so willing to own responsibility? Here is another task for History! With remarkable speed, and on the heels of its own early triumphs, Islam spread like wildfire throughout the lands of north Africa and the Middle East. Few today realise or even want to know that the Middle East had been for over half a millennium the epicentre, the very focal point of Christianity.

Islam changed all that, by invasion and forced conversion (the practice of Dhimmitude), and by limiting access to the holy pilgrimage sites of the Christians. Moreover Saracen armies had invaded Europe reaching as far as the gates of Vienna, their pirates infested the Mediterranean, and in 846 AD they sacked Rome itself.

A further point is worth making about our perception of the Crusades and their aftermath. We in the West, especially those on the left, often suffer the pangs of a guilty conscience over our comparative prosperity and our repression of subject peoples. In so far as we did repress other nations in our colonial past, we should feel guilt. But our prosperity is a relatively new thing, and the colonial and expansionist impetus has not been one-sided. Modern history virtually begins with the conquest of Constantinople by the Muslim armies in 1453. The Ottomans ruled over the Middle East and parts of Europe—even Greece, the birthplace of democracy—for centuries. They were the superpower throughout much of European history.

European nations, particularly in the East, viewed Islam as a threat until virtually modern times. How easy it is to forget that Ottoman Turks were Australia's enemies in the Great War! In setting forth these grievances I do not seek to demean Islam, whose people viewed the task of conversion with the same ardour (if not always employing the same methods) as Christians do. But I insist that these things must be understood before any final judgement is passed on the Crusades. The First Crusade began in 1095, more than 200 years after the Islamic invasion of Italy. One might almost commend the Christian West for the considered slowness of its response!

Thus far I have provided three examples of historical events that have been particularly prone to popular assessment of the most shallow and facile kind, so-called critical and post-colonial theories imposing a biased and one-sided view of history. The least problematic of these is certainly the First World War, for the circumstances that gave rise to it are very well documented, and it was a war fought between nominally Christian Europeans. For that reason it largely escapes denunciations of racism and imperialism that so often skew any discussion on political and social themes nowadays. After all, both sides were arrant colonialists, so what difference does it make who fired the first shots? 'A plague', the PC brigade might well say, 'on both your houses'.

But the other two matters, Slavery and the Crusades, stimulate responses of the most raw and passionate kind and profoundly challenge the West's self-regard. I shall argue that if History is properly practised, or even practised at all (for heaven knows there is little enough of it left in our schools) we will see ourselves as flawed and fallen creatures, capable of deeds of great generosity and kindness, but prone to unspeakable wickedness under pressure of ambition or greed. A great many people are tempted instead to disguise these awful and unpalatable truths under some fatuous doctrine such as 'all men are basically decent', an attitude Geoffrey Blainey nicely described as the 'three cheers' view of history.

And the only way they can uphold such a view is by ascribing all human crime either to one particular group, for example Jews (if we happen to be Nazis) or White European Males (if we subscribe to prevailing post-modern liberal orthodoxy and post-colonial theory), or by blaming 'the system'. How often we hear the system blamed for the failings of men and women! It's the best excuse we can find, and the easiest way to deny the truth that we are all prone to evil deeds if circumstances press us hard enough.

Good history should be a safeguard against this. History is not a science in the sense that Chemistry and Physics are sciences (though it is interesting that the German term Wissenschaft makes no such clear distinction). History does not proceed as the mathematically-based sciences do by the scientific method, making use of experimentation and arriving by iteration at the certainty of proof. But History does deal with objective evidence, or at least claims to do so, and good History seeks to uncover and explain true events with integrity and impartiality, instead of ideology and unproven personal prejudice.

Bad history is an ever-present threat. In its 20 pages, the Australian draft Ancient History curriculum in 2012 mentions religion twice. There was no reference to Christianity anywhere in the document. The Modern History curriculum of the same year was no better: Christianity was simply never mentioned—at least not explicitly. The word religion appeared twice, the first occurrence in the context of Indian history, and the second in the context of Asian and African decolonisation. However the precise phrase in which it is found discloses, I think, the agenda of the compilers: 'the effect of racism, religion and European cultures'. This is an oblique mention of Christianity and a judgement upon it at the same time. This tendentious silence still prevails years later, even after cosmetic changes. The mindset dominates.

Good History's claims are shattered if the possibility of objective knowledge is denied. This brings us face-to-face with History's greatest enemy. Some background is necessary before tackling that. Throughout most of the period of literate civilisation the availability of factual information on any specialised subject has been severely limited and data of any kind has been precious. The hand writing of books, and the great expense of papyrus or parchment, are clearly factors here, but even after the invention of printing libraries remained small by modern standards. During the period of the Enlightenment and into modern times the amount of written information readily available has multiplied beyond all reckoning. Words like mushrooming and escalation cannot come close to describing the enormity of the change from limited availability resources to impenetrable virtual infinitude of material at our disposal.

The chief consequence of this has been the compulsion to specialise, greatly augmented by neo-Marxist critical theory. No one scholar can master his subject any longer. No one specialist can be fully conversant with all the available literature in his speciality. So specialisms arise within specialisms, and the old republic of learning, the common ground that scholars once shared, is a thing of the past, just a dream some of us had.

As an aside, this is less true of some disciplines than of others. Medicine, for example (which ironically almost invented the term specialist) will probably always have a need for general practitioners, individuals so well and thoroughly trained that they have an overview of their whole subject. But by contrast the Arts, including History, have in most places lost all coherence.

Just a few decades ago undergraduate History began with a general study of large tracts of world history before proceeding to broad generalisation in specific areas. Likewise in English students would certainly read several of Shakespeare's plays in their first-year course, as well as a range of novels and poems written over several centuries. Those who chose the works to be studied did so based on recognised and agreed quality. Sometimes poor choices were made which were corrected and adjusted in the course of time, as fashions changed, yet a sense of objective quality, that it was possible to seek out the best thoughts and the best works of the best people, underlay all their endeavours.

Since the Second World War, or thereabouts, the growth of data has had two contrasting consequences. On the one hand scholars whom we may call traditionalists have accepted the situation as they found it, increasingly specialised as the necessity of doing so was thrust upon them but continued to be driven by a sense of objective reality and to believe that truth was a thing to be striven for.

Radicals (to adopt a generic term) on the other hand came to question the very notion of truth: available information was so impossibly impenetrable that truth could never be arrived at, and indeed may not even exist at all. To such thinkers the temptation to view truth as relative became overwhelming: what is true for me may not be true for you, and what is true for you may not be for me.

We all, they would say, have our own truths. I suppose it is fair (and sufficiently generous) to say that the intellectual arm of this kind of thinking is the Post-Modern movement. All this has profoundly impacted the notion of objective truth, for relativism and the subjective view of epistemology make consensus and agreement on anything virtually impossible. Such thinking obviously holds the widest appeal for the materialist who has no kind of belief in a supernatural world, for whom this visible world constitutes the whole of being. Traditionalists by contrast may not always be theists but they generally retain a sense of the absolute, and therefore of the moral and spiritual compass by which alone right actions are discerned.

Having identified, as I hope, the two main divergent consequences of the explosion of knowledge in modern times, let us consider ways in which good History might be reactivated as a useful tool for living. Not as a predictor, in the scientific sense, of future events, but as a means of recognising our place in time, understanding why we are as we are, and suggesting the paths we should follow to achieve maximum fulfilment for ourselves and our nations.

It helps to look at the word itself. History is derived from a Greek word meaning enquiry. We use the word too loosely, in my view, when we talk about 'things that happened in history' as if the word simply means the past. History is an enquiry into the past—or indeed into the present: Thucydides tells how he saw that the war that was then beginning between Athens and Sparta would be a momentous and devastating one and therefore began to record events as they occurred. Even in writing of present events Thucydides was dependent on seeking and gathering evidence—naturally he could not be present at every action in the war—and the result is a narration which purports to tell the whole story of that disastrous conflict, complete with speeches that are confections designed to encapsulate the gist, the spirit, of what he believed was said at the time.

We would today find his methodology flawed, in that regard, but we respect his account as a whole and we sense that he would be at one with us in asserting the existence of absolute truth. Things really happened, whether we know about them or not and, as I began by saying, no individual will ever see the whole picture.

To a Christian none of this should be surprising or disappointing, for Christianity is a surprisingly sceptical faith. We see through a glass darkly: we know very little by means of our own perception, but we trust by means of faith and we hope for the completion of our knowledge and the perfection of our natures. There is something almost Socratic about the Christian's route through the world: we know that we know very little, but we also recognise that there is a boundless body of truth waiting to be revealed in due course.

This is very different from the scepticism of the modern man who denies the objective reality of truth of any kind and believes that we construct for ourselves what passes for truth, which is little better than shorthand for saying that whatever we want (or have been indoctrinated) to believe to be true, is true. This is the world of Walt Disney:

When you wish upon a star,
Makes no difference who you are,
Anything your heart desires
Will come to you.
If your heart is in your dream
No request is too extreme
When you wish upon a star
As dreamers do.

I began by suggesting that I can offer some kind of remedy to counter the trivialising and politicising of History. The remedy is very easily prescribed but will only work for people who are predisposed to take it. That is to say—people who believe that the universe is real and knowable, in practice, by those who troubled to explore it. Children know this instinctively and can be relied upon to become historians for themselves, provided their innocence is not suborned by those of their elders and betters who have imbibed the poison of scepticism. So much of this therefore depends on the availability in schools and universities of non-toxic teachers, a tall order when the trend appears to be in the other direction—towards neo-Marxist inspired critical theory and postmodernism.

But there are signs that things will improve as small liberal arts institutions, like Sydney's Campion College, spring up around the world, as major universities work with organisations such as the Ramsay Foundation to teach solid courses that are not founded on identity politics, and as individuals like the outspoken Jordan Peterson, the late Sir Roger Scruton and the Editor of this anthology dare to question the orthodoxies of political correctness. There is a pretty paradox in that last sentence, by the way: to a sceptic who believes that all truth is relative there is no such thing as orthodoxy!

To conclude, history as commonly taught, if it is taught at all, has been corrupted by relativism which effectively teaches that since we cannot know everything, there is nothing to know. And by the most daring of ironies the cultural-left insist that all history is subjective and relative, while at the same time demanding that students be taught their own dogma that Western Civilisation is riven with racialism and European exceptionalism! The remedy is to ensure that our schools teach History and not just social or gender or race studies. That the latter may in fact be valid fields of studies I do not deny, but they must be preceded by the serious study of as much of the whole sweep of human history as we can manage, so that we have a context and foundation on which to build our specialisations. We have seen that the great Thucydides wrote history (I use the word in its common sense) as it was playing out. We can and should do the same.

If enough of us dare to probe the evidence with the objectivity of scientists we may in time reverse the darkening influence of those who, for example, claim membership of one sex or another (or of neither) without regard to their chromosomes and physical characteristics, or those who identify as 'black' without regard to their ancestry. This identity fixation is evidently too hot for most politicians to handle, so it awaits the courage of more and more ordinary people in schools and universities.

David Daintree's background is in Classics. He has taught Latin, Greek, English and History at secondary and tertiary levels, was master (at various times) of three university colleges, and became the second President of Campion College, Australia's first degree-granting liberal arts institution. In 2013 he founded (under the patronage of the Archbishop of Hobart) the Christopher Dawson Centre for Cultural Studies, of which he is the Director. He has been published from time to time in such journals as Quadrant, *the* Spectator *and the* New Oxford Review, *but devotes most of his writing time to the regular Dawson Centre newsletter. He was made a Member of the Order of Australia in 2017.*

CANCEL CULTURE IN THE TIME OF COVID-19

TONY ABBOTT

Back in 1986, John Howard observed that 'the times will suit me'. They didn't at the 1987 election, but eventually they did, and he went on to become our second longest serving prime minister. As well, he was the first Australian PM to describe himself as a 'conservative', albeit a 'Burkean' one.

With the pandemic still inhibiting daily life and generating almost unimaginable public spending, even from governments of the centre-right, this is a dispiriting time for everyone wanting government that's smaller, tax that's lower and freedom that's greater. Yet even in the face of a pandemic, it remains a fact that government can't spend a dollar that it doesn't raise today or won't pay back tomorrow. And once the fear of disease has passed, people's instinct for freedom will reassert itself.

In the meantime, those with a preference for freedom and a concern for lasting prosperity still have to 'fight the good fight' and perhaps to focus even more on the one main element of conservatism that's not in temporary eclipse, namely love of country, with all that involves: respect for our institutions, pride in our history and faith in our future.

Scott Morrison was right when he said at the start of the pandemic that 2020 could be the worst year of our lives. The challenge is to make sure that it's just one bad year and not the start of a dismal decade or a lost generation. That means trying to learn from this experience rather than entrenching what's unsustainable.

As Health Minister in the Howard government from 2003 to 2007, I massively upgraded the National Medicine Stockpile, including all-but-cornering the world market for anti-viral drugs, in anticipation of a possible bird flu pandemic. Back then, the National Pandemic Plan included early international border closures, special isolation facilities, mobile testing and treatment, and ramped up ICUs. It never included, even in its August 2019 iteration, advice to close state borders, shut workplaces and cancel mass gatherings in a moderate pandemic. Its 'ethical framework' included 'ensuring that the rights of the individual are upheld as much as possible' and 'that measures taken are proportional to the threat'.

Because bird flu had a case fatality rate approaching 50 per cent and because even a readily transmissible pandemic variant was thought likely to be at least as deadly as Spanish Flu, the challenge, I thought back then, would be to keep essential services going—not to order people to stay at home.

It's curious how much of the response to COVID-19 has mimicked the response to the Spanish Flu pandemic of a century ago, with state borders closed, large events banned, hotels and restaurants shut, and compulsory mask-wearing, even though COVID-19 has turned out to be far less dangerous. In Australia, Spanish Flu is thought to have killed about 15,000 people from a population of five million. In America, it killed more than half a million from a population of 100 million. Around the world, it's thought to have killed upwards of 50 million. Unlike now, it was people in their prime who were most at risk.

Then, there was a stoic acceptance that disease was part of life; now, the emphasis is on banishing disease and stoicism is mostly reserved for the restrictions needed to bring this about; even though the health impact of this pandemic, so far, is about as severe as the Asian Flu pandemic of the late 1950s, and the Hong Kong Flu pandemic of the late 1960s, which both had well over a million deaths worldwide without triggering anything approaching large-scale shutdowns.

My sense is that it's the seismic cultural shifts, now underway in the West, that have driven a pandemic response that's so different from that envisaged under plans drawn up even just a short time ago. We are materially rich but spiritually poor, and generally more fearful. More self-confident governments would not have placed so much faith in unelected and unaccountable experts. The experts would not have so readily changed their minds about needing mandatory shutdowns. Societies that retained more 'faith in the world to come' would have been less alarmed by a virus like those that have readily been seen off before.

Governments have become almost neurotic about after-the-event accusations of doing 'too little too late' so instead tend to do 'too much too soon' —to rush to eliminate risk rather than to mitigate it. And social media has exacerbated people's tendency to lose perspective on the latest threat, whatever it might be.

Yes, but for the social-distancing measures put in place, this pandemic could have been worse. Even so, it's not realistic to subsidise wages and businesses indefinitely, to shut venues whenever cases spike, and to keep borders closed in the absence of a vaccine that still can't be counted on—or could take years to become universal; because at some point people will start to count the costs of COVID-19 against the costs of the measures to deal with it. This may already have happened in parts of America, which seem to be managing the virus rather than trying to suppress it, let alone eradicate it.

For all governments—at all times—the challenge is to get the balance right between keeping people safe and keeping people free. The way we have expressed this in Australia has been to try to give everyone a 'fair go' without restricting individuals' ability to 'have a go'. The pandemic has presented all governments with invidious choices, but especially conservative ones that are normally intent on minimising official intrusions into people's daily lives.

Largely thanks to the early closure of our international borders, Australia has been remarkably successful in minimising COVID-19 deaths; but with $300 billion currently committed, essentially paying people not to work, at what cost to our 'have a go' spirit, especially given that finding people to fill jobs—thanks to the higher dole—has become harder than ever?

It's been instructive to compare the pandemic responses of the Victorian Labor government and the NSW Liberal National one. It's hard to discern any health justification at all for the curfew and the 'ring of steel' around Melbourne. At times, Labor premiers have seemed almost to revel in closing their borders, restricting their businesses, and giving orders to the public. The pandemic has been a plausible rationale for much the bigger and more interfering government that voters would normally reject. The Liberal premiers, on the other hand, certainly NSW' Gladys Berejiklian, have been reluctant health despots. Their emphasis has been on keeping the economy open as far as possible.

There's no doubt that ordering people to stay at home for long enough can stop infectious disease in its tracks, as Victoria has shown. But while the memories of this pandemic are fresh, and well before the next one arrives, different potential strategies from attempted eradication, to suppression, to management need much further study and public debate. To what extent should everyone be locked down in order to protect a vulnerable minority; and is there a better option than locking up the elderly on the one hand or exposing them to premature death on the other, because selective shielding was too hard to manage?

When the Italian hospital system seemed to be collapsing under the strain of COVID-19 cases, a degree of public panic was understandable. But nine months on, with the virus much better understood and much less likely to kill, it's still being treated like the grim reaper. More perspective on this virus, at least going forward, could help to dispel the climate of fear that, once created, is hard to shake, and that tends to bring out the authoritarian in officials and the conformist in citizens.

Every death is sad but is a coronavirus death any more tragic than a death from cancer, heart disease, traffic accident or suicide? Every day in Australia nearly 500 people can be expected to die from various causes, some preventable, including about 150 people in nursing homes. Provided governments can prevent the health system from collapsing under the COVID-19 strain, and can protect the most vulnerable in nursing homes, what extra social and economic costs should they impose? The answer can't be none; but it can hardly be whatever it takes either.

Although conservatism is pragmatic, it's still a pragmatism based on values. Even for public safety, centre-right governments are reluctant regulators and cautious spenders. What's important now, if conservatism is not to suffer a serious loss of morale and crisis of conviction, is to wind all this back as quickly as possible and to try to ensure that the response to the next pandemic is a more sustainable balance between suppressing the disease and suppressing normal life.

'We're all in this together' has been the pandemic's background chorus, but that hasn't been people's everyday experience. Public servants and politicians have had their pay maintained or even increased, while working from home. While the JobKeeper wage subsidy has lasted, some workers earned far more than usual, but with less actual need to work; while many others took a 20 per cent pay cut. Thanks to government decision-making, many business owners saw their income slashed, but not their expenses.

Current good polls for most incumbents notwithstanding, I doubt that the public's 'better safe than sorry' initial response to this lost year will survive much reflection. When state governments get away with imposing tougher restrictions on churches than on brothels and on religious services than on sporting events, keeping state borders closed for months longer than any health imperative could justify, requiring people on the street to produce their 'papers' in order to avoid heavy fines, denying sick and dying people ready access to their families because of minute infection risk, failing to notice storm-trooper tactics against people in parks or in their own homes, and announcing draconian new restrictions based on impossible-to-question 'expert advice' (that's invariably not released), public trust is unlikely to be sustained.

The unity that the National Cabinet was supposed to symbolise and engender lasted only as long as the initial lockdown that the federal government almost entirely had to pay for. On state border re-openings, school resumptions, and business freedom, there's been a states' veto over national leadership, even if it might have been worse without the PM's steadying influence. Our sense of nationhood could take a long time to recover from the Queensland Premier's declaration that 'Queensland hospitals are for Queenslanders'; or the West Australian Premier's refusal to allow Australians from other states to enter his, even with quarantine.

Trying to avoid partisan rancour in a time of crisis should not preclude pointing out obvious paradoxes, such as state governments legislating in favour of assisted suicide for people with limited life expectancy at the same time as society is at least partially shut down to stop very old and sick people from succumbing to COVID-19. It's a strange moral order where dying of natural causes is a tragedy that government has a duty to prevent but killing yourself is a right that government has a duty to provide for.

Always, it's the job of a thoughtful conservative to question and to doubt; to insist that new measures be justified, and proportionate, especially when change goes counter to considered positions that conservative political movements have been supporting for decades. Of course, as Cicero once declared, 'the people's safety is the highest law' but that hardly makes 'safety first' the only principle, or even the first principle that should guide government.

Especially when the impact of action or inaction is speculative and when not knowing the future makes it hard to decide what to do now; it's more important than ever not to over-react. Even if Australia's COVID-19 toll remains low and there's a quick recovery from the policy-induced economic slump; even if an early vaccine means that Australia does not need to remain closed to the world, this is unlikely to be a time anyone recalls with much pride because so much that's happened has been out of character with an Australia accustomed 'to strive, to seek, to find and not to yield'.

Not only will the Australia that emerges from the pandemic have more debt, higher unemployment and bigger, more-intrusive government; it's likely to be more lost about what holds us together as a nation and more confused about the things we value.

The pandemic has coincided with a renewed assault on our history as fundamentally racist, and requiring atonement, despite the fact that

Australia became a magnet to migrants, eventually from all over the world, even while it was still a penal colony. It can't have been lost on anyone concerned about political correctness and the cancel culture that police in Victoria failed to make a single arrest when 10,000 people marched for Black Lives Matter; but made 400 arrests at a much smaller protest against ongoing health restrictions. Yet almost nothing was made of this double standard; partly because the leaders who would normally notice it were preoccupied with the pandemic and trying to make a national cabinet work.

As well as habituating people to accept restrictions on freedom and massive government spending 'for our own good', the pandemic seems to have accelerated the elevation of opinion over fact and how we feel about things over what actually happened. We know that Aboriginal people had inhabited Australia for tens of thousands of years prior to British settlement. Post 1788, their society was disrupted and their population devastated, mostly by disease, occasionally by violence. They weren't always given a vote. They didn't always get the same wage. They didn't always get the same justice.

But we also know that Captain James Cook appreciated the qualities of the Aboriginal people he found; that the British government enjoined Governor Arthur Phillip to 'live in amity' with the native people; that Philip refrained from vindictiveness or punitive measures as a matter of policy, even after he had himself been speared at Manly; and that white men were hanged for the murder of blacks as early as the 1830s after the Myall Creek massacre. We also know that massive efforts have been made to give Aboriginal people a better life, first by missionaries and later by government.

It's true that Aboriginal people are hugely over-represented in our jails, even now. But that's because they're heavily over-represented in our courts and crime statistics; as are all people who don't finish school, don't have jobs and live in dysfunctional households. At least as much as some belated measure of recognition in the Constitution, Aboriginal people need to go to school and to take jobs at the same rate as other Australians, for reconciliation to be complete.

In the end, cancel culture is not about correcting a particular injustice or righting a particular historical wrong. It denies moral legitimacy to the whole Australian project, just as it also does in the United States and Britain. You can argue that things could have been done better and that more must be done now; but it's hard to maintain that British settlement should not have happened; or that, on balance, it wasn't a golden moment in human history.

On balance, it was a blessing that the British settled Australia. It's hard to imagine a contemporary Portuguese, Spanish or French governor declaring, as Phillip did, that there could be 'no slavery in a free land'. Even in those days, it was the Royal Navy that was doing its best to extirpate the West African slave trade to the Americas.

There are now calls for a pandemic-triggered 'great reset' from the globalist establishment. This won't just mean entrenching bigger government and much higher public spending. It will also involve a new push for a drastic rethink of institutions that have stood the test of time. In Australia, this always translates into agitation to change our flag and to remove the crown from our constitution.

Yet it's dead wrong to see only the flag of another country (albeit our founder) within our own, rather than the crosses of St Patrick, St Andrew and St George representing our Christian heritage; or to neglect the symbolism of the Southern Cross with its significance to indigenous people. It's wrong to focus on a 'foreign monarch' when that Crown—and the ideals of duty and service that we have assimilated— has been with us every step of our journey as a nation. Besides, it's vandalism to demolish anything when there's nothing better to replace it with; and it's arrogance in any one generation to think that its collective wisdom wholly surpasses that of every predecessor.

Our response to the Black Lives Matter protests was too apologetic. Instead of looking the other way while their statues were graffitied, we should have resolved to end the neglect of people like Cook and Phillip because, without them, there would have been no Australia. Cook was a scientist and a humanist, as well as one of the greatest explorers in all history. Phillip didn't so much found a penal colony as begin a nation, whose freedom, fairness and prosperity quickly became the envy of the world.

Instead of empathising with the would-be statue toppers, there should be a renewed emphasis on the wondrous legacy of the English-speaking version of Western civilisation: including the world's common language, the industrial revolution, the mother of parliaments, and the emancipation of minorities. That perspective is at least as worthy of permeating the national school curriculum as the currently ordained Indigenous, sustainability and Asian ones.

And if there are too many statues to by-gone imperial potentates, let's add a few more to those who should be Australian icons: to Sir John Monash, for instance, the Jewish citizen-solider, hailed as 'the most resourceful general in the British Army', who broke the stalemate on the Western Front and helped to deliver victory in the Great War; and to Lord Florey, the inventor of penicillin, that's saved literally hundreds of millions of lives.

And if there's too many 'dead, white males', let's enlarge our history, not rewrite it and be less blinkered about those who have made a difference: people like Neville Bonner, for instance, the first Indigenous member of the Australian parliament; and Dame Enid Lyons, our first female cabinet minister; neither of whom, as yet, seem to have statues in their honour.

The pandemic will pass. What should never pass is respect for the people and the institutions that have made modern Australia. The economy will never be unimportant because there can be no society without an economy to sustain it. But post-pandemic, conservatives are likely to be patriots first and economic reformers second. One thing the pandemic has helped to clarify is the new fault line in politics, not between those who want bigger and those who want smaller government but between those who are proud of our country and those who can't help wanting to remake it.

To me, as much as the fashion for 'government-knows-best' and magic pudding economics, the most vexing aspect of these COVID-19 times is the aversion to almost any risk. The daily drum beat of infections and deaths, the constant stress on obeying the rules, has gone beyond accommodating people's fears to the point of playing on them. I can't recall a time when Australians have been expected to be grateful for getting some freedoms back, such as having 20 rather than ten visitors to your home; so focussed on merely existing over really living; or so set on prudence over courage. After all, it shouldn't be the prospect of death that scares us so much as a failure to have lived fully in the meantime.

It's easy enough to spotlight COVID-19 infections and deaths. It's much harder to capture mental health issues or the numbers of jobs lost and businesses closed by policies to keep the plague at bay, or the general timidity that's being fostered, yet that deserves attention too. It can't just be assumed that inaction always costs more than action; and that the cure is never worse than the disease. The risk that any action might make a bad situation worse has to be considered too.

Always, the Australian preference has been for people who made things happen and who got things done. Our heroes were those who'd meet challenges, rather than sidestep them. For premiers much more on centre-stage than usual; for health officials dictating the terms of daily life; and above all, for the scientists seeking COVID-19 cures, these are the most bracing of times. For everyone else, though, there's been the dull prospect, not of doing more but of doing less: not 'how much more can I do for my country' but 'how much less must I do in order to be safe'. Strange times indeed.

I can't think of a better way to improve than resolving not to be dominated by a virus; with a renewed emphasis on the active virtues and the robust attitudes that have made Australia a country to be proud of, where sympathy for the weak, encouragement for the underdog and openness to the wider world jostle with scepticism about orthodoxies and a preference for fact over speculation. Let's get back to being people who 'have a go', so that 2020 turns out to be the only year in our history blighted by a focus on what we can't do, rather than what we can. Of course, our best days are ahead of us; but only if we're determined to make the most of ourselves and build on our strengths.

Tony Abbott is the 28th Prime Minister of Australia and a former Health Minister. He's the author of four books, most notably Battlelines, *and frequently contributes to newspapers and magazines. Currently, he's an advisor to the British Board of Trade, a fellow of the IPA, and on the board of the Ramsay Centre for Western Civilisation.*

SLOUCHING TOWARDS GROUPTHINK: CANCEL CULTURE, THE LAW AND RELIGION

JOHN STEENHOF

Mrs May winced. She thought the word, Jesus, should be kept inside the church building like other words inside the bedroom. She was a good Christian woman with a large respect for religion, though she did not, of course, believe any of it was true.

Flannery O'Connor, *Greenleaf* in *Everything that Rises Must Converge* (1965)

Introduction

In her short story, *Greenleaf*, Flannery O'Connor wryly observes the prevailing attitude towards Christianity of the privileged classes in the deep South of the USA. Sixty years on, the cultural seeds that O'Connor discerned of distaste and hostility for religion in the US have come to full bloom in many Western nations, including Australia.

In Australian society, Jesus is being increasingly told to stay inside the church building. More and more, religious Australians—particularly Christians—are under attack for openly living out their faith and are increasingly being excluded from the public square.

While Australians profess a tolerance for religion, a great proportion of them don't believe it to be true and certainly don't want Christians to speak about it. This can be seen in the research. A 2019 survey by the ABC called The Australia Talks National Survey confirms that 71 per cent of Australians hold the view that religious discrimination happens occasionally or often. Australians recognise that religion generally gets a raw deal. Yet, most of those same people – 60 per cent of Australians according to the ABC survey – would prefer that people keep their religious views to themselves. Keep religion in the church, the synagogue and the mosque. Keep your beliefs in your head.

This general antipathy towards religion is shared and fuelled by Australia's cultural elites and the political and media class. In late 2019, retired High Court justice the Honourable Justice Michael Kirby AC CMG wrote a letter complaining the Australian Law Journal published too many articles that supported a proposed Federal law to protect religious people from discrimination.

In his letter, Kirby invokes 'the common conviction that religion in Australia is basically a private matter best kept out of the public zone' and surmises that legal protection of religious freedoms will lead to nastiness and hostility by religious Australians that society can well do without. Kirby suggests most Australian citizens and members of the legal profession share his views.

While Kirby is unlikely to be sufficiently familiar with everyday Australians to speak for them, he is certainly qualified to opine about the legal profession. Indeed, the attitudes of the wider Australian cultural authorities who control the institutions—including the media, the public service sector and much of corporate Australia—are antagonistic to religion and atheistically secular—they believe a secular society is not one in which the church participates, but one in which the church is banished from participation in the public square. There is an increasing cultural prejudice against religion and especially Christianity, which has been one of the key battlegrounds of the culture wars.

A bedrock of a healthy liberal democratic society is the freedom to exchange ideas and express beliefs and to participate in public debate. A society that lacks such freedoms will not last for long. In many sectors of the public square today, however, merely being exposed to an idea you disagree with is increasingly seen as harmful and dangerous.

As the cultural-left gains ascendancy and control of key institutions in Australia, these culture wars over freedoms of thought, conscience and belief have taken on a legal dimension. Increasingly, Australian laws are being weaponised to silence religious voices and to cancel religious Australians who express ideas that are discordant with the atheistically secular ideological fashions of the day. But to silence those ideas by legal means is a direct attack on a flourishing pluralistic society and will inevitably lead to enforced groupthink and thought policing.

To date, much of this legal action has been confined to the public square and the workplace. But worryingly, laws are now being passed in state and territory legislatures that will extend the reach of cancel culture into the private lives of Australians.

Freedom of religion is particularly vulnerable to cancel culture that uses lawfare—the process of attempting to coerce or punish a person's actions through litigation. While religious freedom is widely recognised as a fundamental and inalienable right in international law, it has little express protection in Australia law. In 2018, the Ruddock Religious Freedom Review reported to the Government about deficiencies in Australian law. Progress has stalled on a rather modest Federal Bill to provide limited protection against religious discrimination which was circulated in 2019 but has been on the backburner since.

Australia is a signatory to the International Covenant on Civil and Political Rights which includes protection for religion in Article 18 as a fundamental right that accompanies the essential freedoms of thought, speech, conscience and association.

The religious freedoms protected by the ICCPR are broad and wide ranging—the right to hold to religious beliefs without interference, to express those beliefs publicly and privately, and to practice religion individually and in community with others. The freedom to engage in religious activity can only be subject to necessary restrictions as necessary to protect public safety or the rights of others.

Yet, Australian law provides scant safeguards for these rights. The section of the Australian constitution that protects religious freedom has been essentially nullified by our Courts, and most states and territories only have modest protections against religious discrimination. These protections largely consist of a patchwork of 'exceptions' or 'exemptions' to discrimination laws. These exemptions are an illogical and terrible way to protect an important positive right and give the impression that religious Australians are given preference to discriminate where other people are prohibited from doing so. It perpetuates a narrative that Christians are bigots and given special licence for bigotry. Atheistic secularists and the coterie of cultural-left lobbyists have been involved in a concerted campaign to remove these exceptions from law for many years.

Religious freedom is a right as important as any other and should have positive and explicit protections that take religiously-motivated belief and conduct out of the category of discrimination altogether.

The primary way that Australian law currently 'protects' religious freedom is by the absence of laws. Generally, the reason you can go to a synagogue, wear a cross around your neck at work or wear a burqa in public is because there are no laws that stop you from doing these things.

These are fragile protections because there is little to prevent the enactment of laws that restrict religious freedom and very few legal grounds for defending against the misuse of laws to suppress and stifle unpopular Christian expression. It is worth looking in more detail at how this encroachment of hostile laws plays out in the public square, in the workplace and in the private sphere.

In the public square: vilification laws

In many states in Australia, vilification laws make it an offense to carry out acts that might incite hatred, revulsion, or ridicule of a person with particular attributes, such as sexual orientation or gender identity. These laws appear beneficial on the surface. Who wouldn't object to hatred or ridicule of vulnerable people?

In Australia, activists are increasingly misusing these vilification laws to attack people with religious and political convictions that they do not like. The vociferous opposition to attempts to change the vilification provisions of section 18C of the Commonwealth Racial Discrimination Act have put a spotlight on the problem of using offense as a basis for cancel culture. The failure of the modest changes proposed to section 18C has also shown how dedicated the cultural-left is to preserving tools of oppression in the current laws about vilification.

Vilification laws have particular flaws that make them ripe for abuse. They set a low bar for successful complaints and allow complainants to drag people before Commissions and Tribunals to challenge reasonable speech while alleging purely hypothetical harms. Key flaws of vilification laws include:

- The standard is low—a complainant merely has to show hypothetical incitement to 'ridicule' or to cause 'offence'.
- A person doesn't have to have intent to vilify—a person could unwittingly vilify someone and face penalty.
- Harm is irrelevant—a complaint can be brought regardless of whether that person actually suffered ridicule or hatred.
- Remoteness is irrelevant—no link between a person complaining and the supposed vilification is necessary. An activist in Sydney can complain about a public comment made in Cairns; and
- Truth is generally irrelevant—if a person makes a true statement, that is no defence to a claim of vilification if that truth will incite ridicule.

In many cases, the commissioners and officers deciding these vilification claims are members of an elite class of society that is uniform in socio-political viewpoint. They are part of a privileged administrative class that is so isolated from the public that there is serious doubt that they are able to determine what is likely to be speech that incites ridicule or revulsion.

Vilification laws place a chokehold on freedom of speech and give activists a method to co-opt the law as an adjunct to the social media mobs and speech police that are the usual tools in the cancel culture arsenal.

Examples abound of the misuse of vilification laws, including the prominent case of Tasmanian Archbishop Julian Porteous who was on the receiving end of a vilification complaint in 2017 when he distributed a pamphlet drafted by the Catholic Bishops of Australia in Tasmanian Catholic Schools in support of the traditional Catholic doctrines of marriage during the marriage postal survey. The Archbishop's case gained substantial media attention and although the claim was eventually dropped, it served its purpose—to stifle speech that opposed changes to the marriage laws.

But there are less high-profile cases as well. Early in 2020, Queensland professional photographer and mother-of-four Katrina Tait faced a worthless vilification claim made against her by a Sydney activist.

Katrina had posted on Facebook in support of a public petition to remove a Drag Queen Story Time event from Brisbane public libraries—where drag queens read LGBTIQ+ picture books to little children. In her post, Katrina remarked that adult entertainers were not good role models for young children and should not be reading stories to them.

A homosexual activist in Sydney and prolific litigator made a claim against Katrina with the NSW Anti-Discrimination Board alleging that this Queensland post about a local Brisbane issue was insulting and incited ridicule against homosexuals. The Board refused to reject this clear attempt to pursue someone out-of-state with an ideologically motivated claim. As is often the case, the complaint was withdrawn. However, the effect of such a stressful ordeal for ordinary Australians cannot be underestimated. The process is often the punishment in these kinds of weaponised vilification claims.

A flourishing democratic society requires a robust debate of competing ideas. The abuse of vilification laws by viewpoint activists is not only detrimental to free speech, but it is also detrimental to a healthy liberal democratic society. A civil society should not allow the law to be used to attack people because of their ideas. It should listen and engage in the pursuit of truth—no matter how disagreeable or politically incorrect—for the benefit of all.

In the workplace: codes of conduct

Increasingly, the employment contracts of the Australian worker are being supplemented with Codes of Conduct that purport to regulate the behaviour and speech of employees, not just at work but also in their own personal time. These Codes usually include high-sounding statements about respect for tolerance, diversity and inclusion which are often used to opposite effect to hound those whose ideas do not conform to the fashionable cultural-left zeitgeist.

These Codes of Conduct often have the force of law for workers, and present fertile ground for activists to weaponise those codes to attack speech they don't like—in particular, religious speech.

In 2019, the case of rugby player Israel Folau—who played for Australia—burst onto the nation's consciousness. The case is well known. Folau was unlawfully dismissed by the Australian Rugby Union for his personal Instagram post sharing his Christian faith and quoting a Bible verse from 1 Corinthians 6:9-11 that was viewed as insulting to homosexuals. Folau was cancelled because of his personal beliefs. After commencing legal action, the Australian Rugby Union eventually settled the case and gave Folau a large payout. Folau no longer plays for the Australian national team and instead is playing club rugby in Europe.

What is less well-known is the practical implications of Folau's case for religious freedom. Sekope Kepu (another Christian rugby player in the Wallabies) prepared a statement in support of Folau's case documenting the fallout of Folau's exit from the team. Kepu spoke about how the Christians in the team felt marginalised and how management prevented players from speaking to the media in support of Folau. Most interestingly, Folau's termination led to a chilling of the religious expression of other players in the team. Kepu states:

Israel was important to me as a Christian member of the teams. After Israel moved to rugby in 2013, he helped me feel more confident in expressing my religion in front of the playing groups.

Before Israel started, two or three of us Christian players would pray before games hiding in a corner. I lacked confidence to show my faith, thinking that other players might view us as 'weirdos' for being religious.

Israel also started team prayer groups the night before each game. Any player could join if they wanted ... Since Israel has been gone the prayer groups have stopped.

Kepu gives a revealing insight into the hidden consequences of the Folau case. The persecution of Folau was effective to silence other religious members of the Wallabies and to make clear that they are going to have to self-censor and pay lip-service to fashionable ideology or face a similar fate to Folau.

The threat is not just to sports players. Doctors and other health professionals are increasingly being forced to align with a cultural-left agenda through creeping limits imposed by Codes of Conduct. Breach of the Code can lead to doctors being struck-off by the Medical Board.

The Medical Board is increasingly kerbing doctors' freedoms by importing leftist critical theory concepts about issues like cultural safety, white supremacy and colonisation into the Code of Conduct.

Vague terminology allows the Medical Board to ideologically interpret Codes of Conduct to cancel unpopular beliefs and enforce leftist groupthink. This is the politicisation of the medical profession. The medical profession is not a forum for Medical boards to bring culture wars—people's physical health and wellbeing should be paramount. A health regulator should not be able to dictate a medical practitioner's politics or religious beliefs, especially in relation to controversial and sensitive issues like late term abortion, euthanasia and transgender procedures. It is deeply concerning that one of the changes to the Code requires a medical practitioner to acknowledge systemic racism in providing care.

A regulator should not be able to compel speech and should not police the personal political or religious convictions of doctors. The Australian Medical Association, hardly a bastion of conservative thought, has made the following comment about the Code: 'It would be unprecedented for a regulatory authority's Code of Conduct to attempt to control a doctor's public expression of opinion in a context which may not impact on the standard or quality of direct patient care or the wider health system nor reflect a lack of medical professionalism'.

No one knows this better than Dr Jereth Kok, a Victorian GP with 13 years' experience who in 2019 was the target of discipline by the Medical Board for his conservative and religious social media posts.

In 2018, following an anonymous complaint, the Medical Board began investigating Dr Kok's internet posts without his knowledge. In August 2019, the Medical Board gave Dr Kok notice that they proposed to take immediate action to suspend his licence to practice medicine because of his posts and gave him less than a week to prepare for a hearing. At the hearing, Dr Kok was suspended in advance of a full investigation or formal hearing on the basis that it is in 'the public interest' that immediate action was taken.

This is despite the fact that no patient has ever complained about Dr Kok and there has never been any issue with how he practices medicine. On appeal, the Victorian Tribunal upheld the Medical Board's decision.

Dr Jereth Kok is a good doctor. He does his job well. He treats his colleagues well. He treats his patients well. But none of that matters. Solely on the basis of his internet posts, this good doctor's career has been ruined. This happened not because Dr Jereth did the wrong thing but because Dr Jereth said the wrong thing—and all originating from an anonymous complaint from an activist. Another example of cancel culture by way of the legal system.

Decisions like these show the dangerous encroachments being made on freedom of speech. The Tribunal that confirmed Dr Kok's penalty observed that he has 'clear conservative leanings' and he expressed his views strongly. The problematic posts related to abortion, sexuality and transgender issues and were out of step with prevailing elite ideology on these issues. The Tribunal considered that there is a risk that Dr Kok's convictions on these matters might bleed into his practice.

Administrative thought-policing has the effect of silencing a diversity of opinions within the medical profession and replacing open discourse and viewpoint diversity with a thin and shallow ideological conformism. In Dr Kok's case, the activist complainer could have engaged with Dr Kok's ideas instead of complaining to the Medical Board. They did not.

The best way to respond to bad ideas is with good ideas. This allows viewpoint diversity and prevents bad ideas from becoming orthodoxy simply because those who have competing ideas are erased. The complainants did not engage with ideas but instead chose to attack Dr Kok's career.

Cancel culture is alive and well in the workplace, and Codes of Conduct are the legal tool increasingly being used as the weapon of choice. But there are increasing threats in the private sphere as well.

In the private sphere: conversion therapy laws

The latest attempt to enshrine cancel culture into law is in the form of Australian state and territory laws which criminalise the practice of conversion therapy. These laws target practices or treatments aimed at changing the sexual orientation, gender identity or expression of people who identify as LGBTIQ+ – in particular, children. In 2019, Victorian Premier Daniel Andrews stated, 'This bigoted quackery masquerades as healthcare … it should be about inclusion and acceptance and valuing people for who they are'.

When the average person thinks about 'conversion therapy' they think of aversion therapies and forms of abuse like beatings, electric shocks, restraints and verbal abuse. On their face, laws prohibiting such barbaric practices would appear beneficial and desirable. Most Australians would think these treatments are terrible and that opposition to such laws would be odious. How do such laws threaten freedoms or legislate cancel culture?

The devil is always in the detail. There is near universal acceptance that coercive and aversive therapies to change a person's sexual desires are wrong and immoral. But in every case in Australia, conversion laws go far beyond criminalising medical treatments that employ aversion therapy. Instead these laws amount to legislated ideology and empower the police to cancel those who do not subscribe to contested theories about sexuality and gender identity.

One of the main problems with conversion laws is that they are a solution in search of a problem: there is no evidence that such therapies are practised in Australia. In a pattern that is becoming familiar, cultural-left activists have confected an outrage to push for legislation to address an illusory problem. No one actually practices aversion therapy. There is not some epidemic of conversion therapy in Australia that has ever been exposed or demonstrated.

The key danger of conversion laws is that they are so broad and vague that they reach into the private sphere and put everyday Australians in the potential firing line—parents, teachers, counsellors and clergy. Because conversion practices (that are being made illegal) are poorly defined in these laws they extend far beyond coercive therapies to criminalise body-affirming treatments, counselling for unwanted sexual desires and talk therapies that explore questions, issues and personal history. Basic forms of mainstream Christian practices such as prayer, scripture reading, spiritual guidance and preaching are directly targeted and encompassed within the ban.

Examples of conduct that Conversion laws could criminalise include:

- Parents. If a 5-year-old biological girl tells her parents that she wants to be a boy, criminal proceedings could be brought against her parents, school, teachers and doctors if they continue to treat her as a girl, counsel her to love the body she was born with, explore alternative reasons other than gender confusion for this expressed desire, or if they adopt a 'watchful waiting' approach in relation to these desires. These are potential practices that could be criminalised as unlawful and harmful attempts to alter or suppress the child's gender identity.

- Teachers. Criminal proceedings for conversion practices could be brought against a Christian school that teaches the orthodox Christian belief that sexuality should only be expressed between a man and a woman within the confines of heterosexual marriage, and that this is normative for Christians.

- Religious Leaders. A Christian pastor leading a Sunday School class of 13-year-olds and explaining the Bible's teaching that homosexual practice is not consistent with Biblical doctrine and that all Christians are called to abstinence and celibacy outside of heterosexual marriage could be criminalised.

- Counsellors. A psychologist examining whether a 14-year-old biological girl's desire to transition to a boy might be related to their autism or arise as a result of sexual trauma would be at risk of criminal sanctions.

Further, the only protected treatments in conversion laws are for treatments that affirm LGBTIQ+ attractions, support gender transition or provide gender transition services (including prescriptions of puberty blockers, hormones and performance of body-invasive surgeries).

Neither is there evidence that links depression, suicide, self-esteem or social isolation with body-affirming counselling—talk therapy that explores questions, issues and personal history to better understand and address unwanted sexual attraction or manage gender dysphoria and confusion.

On closer inspection, these conversion laws that are increasingly being put forward in Australia are a Trojan horse, effectively putting in place more tools for legal cancel culture, this time in ways that will extend well into the private sphere. Such laws are a gross overreach and undermine important institutions of Australian society like the church and the family.

Such conversion laws intrude unnecessarily and disproportionately with fundamental freedoms of individuals, parents, teachers and religious leaders and undermines the rights of family, rights of freedom of religion and rights of freedom of expression in a disproportionate way.

Conversion laws plant ticking time bombs in Australian law that will explode to cancel those who hold conservative convictions on issues of sexuality and anyone who contests extreme transgender ideology, not just where these ideas are expressed in public, but also where they are taught in the home or preached in the church.

This is compelled ideology, forcing everyone down a pathway of affirmation of homosexuality and transgender identities. There will be a chilling effect on robust challenge and discussion of highly contestable theories that are passed off as 'settled science'. It will prevent those struggling with unwanted desires or questions of identity from exploring a full range of options and will rob parents and children of the ability to obtain full advice and counsel.

Even without a single person facing trial or going to jail, conversion laws give tribunals, police and prosecutors powers of investigation, intimidation and harassment which will effectively coerce compliance with cultural-left ideology and lead to an erosion of the fundamental freedoms of thought, speech and conscience that underpin a vibrant and free society.

Conclusion

These clear threats in the public square, the workplace and the private sphere, brings to mind the lines from the poem *The Second Coming* by William Butler Yeats:

The best lack all conviction, while the worst
Are full of passionate intensity.

Laws that enable cancel culture construct a social environment where the best cannot legally have convictions and must pay lip service to the passionate intensity of the worst. The clear intent of this misuse of Australian laws is to try and erase unpopular convictions and politically incorrect religious beliefs from expression in the public square.

The risk is that Australia becomes a society where people self-censor about their sincere beliefs. This eventually leads to a culture of heavily policed thought and a removal of one of the pillars of a just and flourishing culture. As Yeats concludes his poem:

And what rough beast, its hour come round at last,
Slouches towards Bethlehem to be born?

The rough beast that is the slouching progeny of cancel culture is a society of mandated opinions, excoriated religion and tepid groupthink. Such a society will not last long unless there is a firm cultural rejection of cancel culture and a better balance struck in law to adequately protect fundamental freedoms of speech, conscience and religion.

John Steenhof is the principal lawyer at the Human Rights Law Alliance, a not-for-profit law firm based in Canberra. HRLA is an independent law firm that specialises in religious freedom, and freedom of thought, speech and conscience. John has twenty years' experience working in law firms both large and small in Australia and New Zealand and most recently ran his own commercial and litigation firm in Western Australia before coming to HRLA in 2019. Since 2019, HRLA has been representing Christians, churches, schools and religious organisations to promote, protect and preserve their freedom to act in accordance with their convictions and to speak truth in the public square. HRLA regularly acts for clients in religious freedom cases, advises Christians and religious groups on how to preserve their legal rights to act in accordance with their beliefs and advocates at Federal and State level for laws that protect fundamental freedoms of religion, thought, speech and conscience.

DIVIDED WE FALL

ANTHONY DILLON

Introduction

This chapter is about culture wars and cancel culture in the context of Aboriginal Australia. My hope is that some good may come from this chapter by helping those Aboriginal people who are needlessly suffering. I am assuming all Australians, both Aboriginal and non-Aboriginal, are in a position to make or assist in making some positive change to the lives of Aboriginal Australians who are suffering—if they want to. And I believe that most Australians most of the time want to see good outcomes for their Aboriginal brothers and sisters. I say, 'most of the time' because there are times when some non-Aboriginal Australians wane in their enthusiasm to help, for reasons I will discuss later.

So how might this chapter help Aboriginal Australians? I hope that what I write might influence policy making, allocation of funds, or it could influence those who work, directly or indirectly, with Aboriginal people. For those Australians who are far removed from Aboriginal people, you can still play an important role. I hope that this chapter can help you feel comfortable voicing your opinion on Aboriginal affairs in whatever setting you find yourself. You are entitled to state your opinion on the merits of a voice to parliament or a treaty; what constitutes genuine racism and what doesn't; what you think the priorities should be, or any other issue relating to Aboriginal affairs—for the simple reason, that Aboriginal affairs is everybody's business because we are all citizens of one country.

This anthology is about the culture wars, and this chapter is about the fragmentation and separatism that is recklessly pursued by some Aboriginal cultural warriors and their non-Aboriginal fellow travellers. With that in mind, I will discuss what I believe is driving the war—a war that can have no winners, only varying degrees of losers—and some of its consequences, such as cancel culture and the negative outcomes this leads to for Aboriginal people. I will commence by giving a brief overview of the culture wars, then establish the premise that Aboriginal and non-Aboriginal are not much different from one another—there is more to unite than divide us. Next, I will show how rhetoric is used to validate the false narrative that Aboriginal people are vastly different from non-Aboriginal people, which in turn distracts from addressing the actual problems facing Aboriginal Australians. Finally, I will consider what needs to happen to end the culture wars in Aboriginal affairs.

Culture wars: an overview

The culture war is more complex than simply Aboriginal vs. non-Aboriginal. I believe there are in fact two wars. With regard to the first war, which is Aboriginal vs. non-Aboriginal, I believe the culture war is much smaller than it appears as portrayed on social media, some mainstream media, and some classrooms and lecture theatres in academia. I do not deny that there is conflict between some Aboriginal and non-Aboriginal people, nor do I deny the reality of true racism (which can run both ways), but it is minimal. As Thomas Sowell points out, 'racism is alive, but it's on life support'. Contrary to the prevailing politically correct narrative, I believe the majority of Aboriginal and non-Aboriginal Australians get along well.

The second war, which is the bigger war, is an ideological war between two opposing groups, each comprised of both Aboriginal and non-Aboriginal people. The first group see themselves as saviours of Aboriginal people from an assumed racist mainstream Australia (demonised as 'White Australia'). Their well-worn mantra is 'Aboriginal people in 2021 are suffering from the British invasion from more than two centuries ago, with the suffering sustained by racist Australians today'—as seen in the hysteria that follows when an Aboriginal person dies in police custody or in hospital. Protesters suddenly forget that non-Aboriginal people also die in these circumstances at similar rates (or higher). This fact is ignored so they can use the incident as proof that racism is the culprit. Goethe's observation applies here: 'People find what they look for, and they look for what they believe'.

The second group in the culture war, like the first, is comprised of both Aboriginal and non-Aboriginal people. They do not see mainstream Australia as being to blame for the problems facing some Aboriginal people today, or if they do, they do not attribute malicious intent. They want to see an end to poverty, violence, suicide, sexual abuse, and community dysfunction, and believe that jobs and education are the primary solutions—not a preoccupation with apologies, harping on about past injustices, looking for racism around every corner, chasing treaties, or partaking in dumb cancel-culture activity like changing street names, pulling down statues, or virtue signalling by changing the brand name of Coon Cheese. Practical solutions offered by this second group are often dismissed as 'assimilation' or even 'cultural genocide' by the first group.

Similar cultures

One of my very favourite philosophers, Anthony de Mello, states:

We're all the same. You've got a thin veneer of culture that's different, but deep down we're all the same. The same problems are everywhere. The hatred is the same. The conflict is the same. The guilt is the same. The dependence on people's opinions and the emotional dependence on approval are the same. It's exactly the same. Just scrape off the exterior culture, we're all the same.

For over two decades I have been saying something similar: the commonalities between Aboriginal and non-Aboriginal Australians far outweigh the differences. I think if more people realised this there would be less 'us and them', no identity politics and, therefore, no victimhood and culture wars. I am not suggesting that all Australians should be sucked up into one great homogenous culture, but only that people realise that their cultural identity is only one part of who they are. Nor am I suggesting that some Aboriginal people do not have circumstances (such as poor living conditions) that are vastly different to those that most Australians live in. Their circumstances may often be different, but the human condition is the same.

Differences in culture

The foregoing discussion is not meant to suggest that there are no Aboriginal people in this country with a culture that is distinctly Aboriginal or somehow different from mainstream Aussie culture. However, care needs to be taken when considering cultural differences. I agree with my friends Dave and Bess Price who tell me there is a very broad spectrum of 'Aboriginal' cultures in this country. At one end the Aboriginal culture is Aboriginal in name only and is, for all intents and purposes, indistinguishable from that of their white neighbours. Consider the genuine expressions of Aboriginal culture of Bess. She maintains beliefs and ways of thinking which she learnt from her parents, and they from their parents. These beliefs or ways of thinking are generally very different to that of mainstream Australians. However, while maintaining elements of the Aboriginal culture she was raised in, Bess has embraced modern Australian culture and does not see herself as separate from non-Aboriginal Australians; indeed she has had a long marriage to a whitefella, and served as a Minister of the crown in the Northern Territory, serving all Territorians and not just Aboriginal citizens. Like me, she may be caught up in the culture wars, but not by choice. She is not promoting the myth that Aboriginal people are vastly different to non-Aboriginal people, which is what starts and sustains the culture wars. She is on the side of acknowledging and celebrating the commonalities between Aboriginal and non-Aboriginal people as Australians rather than obsessing over alleged differences.

I have stayed in Aboriginal communities where there are very real cultural differences between people. In these communities there are many non-Aboriginal workers and families. They generally get on well with their Aboriginal fellow-community members. Sometimes they need to adapt some behaviours, but they do so from a deep desire to get along with each other. After working in these communities for a few weeks, the non-Aboriginal Australians quickly discover de Mello's truth—just scrape off the exterior and we're all the same. This is a truth I suspect that many Aboriginal people have always known. After visits to remote communities, I am reminded of the words from the Warumpi Band: 'Blackfella, whitefella, yellafella, anyfella. It doesn't matter what your colour, as long as you a true fella'.

Phantom culture

The culture wars are built on the belief (myth) that people who identify as Aboriginal must have a different set of beliefs or way of thinking that sets them apart from non-Aboriginal Australians. This is true for some, but for many, at least in the cities where the culture wars were born, most are, as Dave and Bess Price have stated, culturally indistinguishable from their white neighbours. For the gullible, repeating ad nauseam phrases like 'sovereignty never ceded' are assumed to show strength and reflect a set of beliefs that are uniquely Aboriginal and therefore validate the claim that Aboriginal Australians are vastly different from non-Aboriginal Australians. This is a 'phantom culture', much like a phantom limb—you like to think it's there, but it isn't really.

For many Aboriginal 'leaders' (some for whom the title of leader is dubious) whom I have met, I cannot see in them much evidence of a different way of thinking that is somehow uniquely Aboriginal and prevents them from fully engaging in mainstream Australia. Indeed, they typically engage well in mainstream Australia. Bess Price says that a lot of what we see today is a 'Disneyland variety' culture. And there is nothing wrong with a person who identifies as an Aboriginal person having a culture that is more or less the same as that of the mainstream Australian culture. But I believe it is a problem when there is an insistence that anyone who identifies as Aboriginal must therefore be seen as being vastly (or even moderately) different from their non-Aboriginal neighbour (or parent, or partner, or aunt, or cousin).

While these soi-disant 'Aboriginal leaders' manage to function adequately in modern Australian society without any evidence of a cultural clash or a threat to their 'cultural safety', they claim to represent Aboriginal Australians who they believe struggle in modern Australia because their culture is vastly different from that of non-Aboriginal Australians. And there begins the cultural divide followed closely by the culture war.

Closing the claptrap gap

The insistence that Aboriginal Australians are vastly different to non-Aboriginal Australians has given rise to a whole new vernacular. When people start talking about 'connecting with Country' or 'mother earth' or 'first nation's people' or 'sovereignty' or 'assimilation' or 'institutional racism,' they certainly would appear to be different from those around them. But such phrases are just rhetoric. By 'rhetoric' I mean the use of impressive sounding fuzzy and emotive words or phrases that have no precise meaning but are used to bolster an argument, make an opponent look sinister, or make the one using the rhetoric sound intelligent and morally superior. Such rhetoric is a smokescreen. It is a convenient distraction for those who do not wish to acknowledge the tough problems facing some Aboriginal people like violence, child abuse, unemployment, and unsafe and unclean living conditions. Such rhetoric serves only to veil the real issues impacting on Aboriginal people and hinders their advancement and poisons race relations in this country. It is claptrap. It does not close the gap—in fact, claptrap widens the gap.

Consider a story in *The Australian* in 2015 by Rick Morton which led with, 'Hundreds of billions of dollars have been spent in past decades in attempts to close the gap in Indigenous disadvantage; now, it seems, the only things left to throw into that yawning chasm are platitudes about the shocking state of affairs'. There is no shortage of platitudes in Aboriginal affairs. Morton later rhetorically states: 'When so much effort is expended for apparently so little gain, what is left but rhetoric?' Sadly, rhetoric, a hallmark of Aboriginal affairs, continues.

With rhetoric as their weapon, we have 'born again cultural warriors' emerging who are quick to seize on their Aboriginal ancestry and equally quick to tell us how Aboriginal people are being crushed by white colonisation in 2021. But they don't act alone; there is a plentiful supply of non-Aboriginal people looking for a cause who are quick to 'stand in solidarity' with them. Joining the march for solidarity, academia is jumping on the bandwagon. I am not talking about welcome to country ceremonies, which if done properly have their place. I am talking, to give one example, about the use of trendy, politically correct expressions like 'decolonisation'. So, what is decolonisation? Here are a couple of quotes from the Sovereign Union website:

Until we as First Nations and Peoples decolonise our minds we as Aboriginal people will never truly achieve liberation and our problems we face today will persist. Until our thinking changes we will continue to identify with European culture and undermine and doubt our own culture, the oldest and most sustainably developed culture on earth.

and

One of the basic fundamental facets to achieve true decolonisation, that is, we must learn to decolonise our minds. This essentially means that we must stop thinking like our oppressor and thereby stop trying to fit a round peg in a square hole.

Sadly, this is the sort of rhetoric that gains attention and admiration. As a further example, consider the words of Aboriginal educator, Dr Chris Sarra: 'The most fundamental step is acknowledging our humanity ... our humanity is not being acknowledged and this is so tragically reflected in the sad statistics many of us know too well'. Aboriginal people's humanity is not being acknowledged? Seriously Chris? Which grand gesture would demonstrate to doubters that their humanity is actually being acknowledged? Would such a gesture put food on tables, get kids into schools, and prevent women from being bashed? Sarra and plenty of other Aboriginal people have achieved success despite this alleged lack of 'acknowledgement of their humanity'.

Implications

If disagreements, or even heated arguments, were the only thing to result from the culture wars in the sphere of Aboriginal affairs, that would be fine. I think Aussies generally enjoy a good argument, so long as nobody gets hurt. But unfortunately, people do get hurt, and it's mostly Aboriginal people. There are many ways that the culture wars cause harm to Aboriginal people, but due to space limitation I will briefly discuss just three. They are: compromised health and safety; inculcated fragility and victimhood, deterioration of race relations.

Compromised health and safety

Interactions with Police
The Good Book states that a house divided against itself cannot stand. A modern translation provided by psychologist Mark Leary is: 'getting people to view themselves and members of other groups as members of a larger common group produces more positive attitudes, increases trust and openness, and leads former rivals to treat each other more equally and fairly'. Conversely, seeing others as members of separate groups leads to distancing and conflict. When Aboriginal Australians are encouraged to see non-Aboriginal Australians as the oppressor and as racists, then they may be reluctant to seek or receive help from them.

Consider for example the words of egregious blactivist Amy McQuire, who portrays police as: 'the aggravators, as the unjust people, as the people that you need protection from'. McQuire and others, when seeing either a genuine case of police abusing the powers, or more often a perceived case based on 30 seconds of footage caught on a mobile phone with the first few crucial moments missing, are quick to claim: 'See, this is why we find it hard to trust police'. For people who claim that they don't like to be stereotyped, they sure do like to stereotype others.

If Aboriginal people are led to believe that police are a danger to them, then what if they are in danger and need help? Call the police? Not likely. Naturally, McQuire is slow to mention that very often the worst offenders in treating Aboriginal people badly are, in fact, other Aboriginal people. The high level of violence in Aboriginal communities is well documented. And those Aboriginal people who fail to subscribe to the victim narrative are slandered again and again as 'coconut' (brown outside, white inside) or 'sell-out'. I write from lived experience.

Consider the tragic story of two Aboriginal boys who drowned in the Swan River in Perth in 2018 while being pursued by police. Social media was full of claims that the boys were likely in fear for their lives because they supposedly knew what happens to Aboriginal people in custody. Consider the words of Senator Pat Dodson: 'Since the report of the Royal Commission into Aboriginal Deaths in Custody, nearly 440 Aboriginal people have died in Custody. Without answers, this breeds fear of foul play being at work'.

Statements like this are not helpful. Foul play is when there is no mention of the more than 1600 non-Aboriginal people who died in custody during the same period. Context is crucial. An Australian Government publication, The Health of Australia's Prisoners: 2015, states: 'Indigenous Australians were no more likely to die in custody than non-Indigenous Australians'. Specifically, 'With just over one-quarter (27 per cent) of prisoners in custody being Indigenous, and 17 per cent of deaths in custody being Indigenous, Indigenous prisoners were under-represented'.

With some rare common sense at a time of the tragic deaths of these two boys (that doubtless would have been terribly upsetting), the father of one of the boys was reported on an ABC website as saying: 'A lot of people want to blame other people or whatever, upbringing or the police. But I suppose these young boys, that's their way of having fun and unfortunately it costed them their lives'.

Aboriginal children in out-of-home care

Consider the case of placing Aboriginal children with non-Aboriginal foster carers. If the carers can provide a safe living environment where an Aboriginal child in need of care will be loved and cared for, then there should be no issue with that child being placed with a non-Aboriginal family. I don't care what colour their carers or any other children in the household are. But consider the claim on a government website about the 'The Aboriginal and Torres Strait Islander Child Placement Principle'. It states: 'If no other suitable placement with Aboriginal carers can be sought, children are placed with non-Indigenous carers as a last resort, provided they are able to maintain the child's connections to their family, community and cultural identity'. Mmm, a 'last resort'—does that sound a bit racist?

I don't need to give examples of Aboriginal children in need of out-of-home care who have suffered at the hands of 'kin' because of insistences where culture trumped safety. I have associates who have given me horror stories where placing an Aboriginal child with an extended family member was not in the interests of the child, but it ticked the culture box. I have a friend, a non-Aboriginal woman who has Aboriginal descendants, who tells me of the battles she goes through to gain custody of her Aboriginal granddaughter, but preference is given to the other grandmother, who is Aboriginal. This preference would be fine except for the fact that in the Aboriginal grandmother's home the child is exposed to dangers such as domestic violence, drugs, physical and emotional neglect, an unhygienic living environment, and medical and dental neglect. In these culture wars it is too often the Aboriginal children who stand to lose the most.

Leading Aboriginal thinker, Warren Mundine, when writing in *The Australian* about Aboriginal children's wellbeing, has stated that he did not believe children were being removed unnecessarily—and to stop pussyfooting around where the wellbeing of Aboriginal children is concerned. He further stated that in most of these cases there is genuine concern for the safety of the children and that 'You're looking at family trees where there are five generations of abuse … You are seeing this vicious cycle of abuse continuing'. Yes, for the sake of our children— and they are our children—let's stop pussyfooting around.

Inculcated fragility and victimhood

We're told that use of the term 'part-Aboriginal' (which is what I am), is offensive. Nonsense! We are told that Australia Day is offensive. We are told that stating 'you don't look Aboriginal to me' is offensive. We are told the national anthem is offensive. We are told that golliwogs are offensive. Again, nonsense! I could give many more examples but need only give one—Bill Leak's cartoon showing an irresponsible Aboriginal father not knowing the name of his son. While the 'woke', the Aboriginal victim brigade, the offendarati (a term coined by Bill), and the whinja ninjas went nuts about the cartoon on social media, Australia's highest-ranking Aboriginal police officer, my father, Col Dillon, praised Bill for it. In a long and distinguished career my father has seen it all and instantly recognised the message Bill was communicating.

Bill's cartoon and the other examples I gave are just opportunities to take offence—and notice: offence is always taken, never given. And why is it taken? Because in our modern politically correct woke society, to be offended is to feel special and important—and with the right lawyer, it can be profitable.

But if having a bunch of Aboriginal people shouting they are offended was the only consequence of all this then it would not be such a big problem. It is the pandering to the offended that is the problem. When the brand name of a cheese is changed or someone is taken to the Australian Human Rights Commission (as was the case with Bill Leak), such pandering sends the message, 'You are so fragile that you need protection from a cartoon, words, dates (26 January), and even Coon cheese'. When this happens, enter 'cultural safety', 'diversity toolkits', and 'safe spaces' and the counter-productive story of the oppressor and the oppressed is perpetuated.

I think back to how strong my Aboriginal ancestors must have been to survive the arrival of the British and all that came with it and contrast them with many of today's Aboriginal people. It would appear that both their Aboriginal ancestry and their strength have been much diluted. I got lucky; my Aboriginal grandmother was black, gentle, and strong. Her influence on my father, my uncles, aunties, and cousins, is far reaching. And credit to my Aboriginal grandfather that we inherited some of his toughness. Thankfully, I have met other similar Aboriginal people. They are quiet achievers. They may not be out protesting, but they do make Australia a better country. They aren't out looking to be offended; they are out looking to be helpful.

Deterioration of race relations

Aussies are generally a generous lot—Aboriginals and non-Aboriginals. But when non-Aboriginal Australians are constantly told that they are racist for celebrating Australia Day or bombarded with constant rhetoric like 'white supremacy' or 'white privilege' then don't be surprised if some of their enthusiasm for Aboriginal people begins to wane. Maybe it shouldn't be that way but unless you're a saint it can be difficult to not lose some goodwill some of the time.

For those who delight in promoting the 'white man is evil and the cause of all our problems' mantra, here's an important message for you. While your bright idea might be winning you popularity contests, it might also be costing lives. Imagine being a service provider in health or emergency services for instance. Imagine that being spat on, kicked, sworn at, cursed, or threatened is not a rare event but part of the job. Although it is only a minority of Aboriginal people who engage in such behaviour, if it happens enough, then for all your duty of care as a service provider, the way you respond to members of that group can be tested.

Imagine that one day you encounter an Aboriginal person who genuinely needs assistance, but thanks to past experiences of hearing the 'white man is evil' message, on top of feeling tired, run down, underpaid, and underappreciated, you might be prone to unconsciously compromise your usually high standard of service for that one person. Most times you can get away without any harm taking place. But occasionally factors might combine and the outcome could be lethal. That one person may have to pay the price for the insults of the victim brigade.

Critics will say 'Well then, they shouldn't be in the job'. Well, how about these same critics trade in their 'Black Lives Matter' placards for a police badge or stethoscope? The problem is that every profession has imperfect people. Mistakes due to human error will be made. But to insist that Aboriginal people who die in 'white institutions' do so mostly due to racism, well that lie only continues the cultural wars.

Moving ahead

Hopefully, discussing the problems associated with the Aboriginal culture wars points the way to solving these problems. In case it's not apparent what the solutions are, here is a summary:

- Recognise that the commonalities between Aboriginal and non-Aboriginal people far outweigh any differences. We are all Australians. Programs designed to close the gap should start and end with this fundamental truth.
- Following from the first point, recognise that Aboriginal people are people first and Aboriginal second.
- Instead of lumping all Aboriginal people together according to the dumb rule of 'you're either Aboriginal or you're not', there is a need to distinguish between those Aboriginal Australians who do embrace cultural practices that are significantly different from the mainstream Aussie culture and those Aboriginal Australians who are virtually indistinguishable from your average Aussie.
- Embrace the idea that Aboriginal affairs is everyone's business.
- Don't assume that the claim of hurt feelings and offence is an indicator of genuine suffering of Aboriginal people.

Achieving this will require strong leadership at all levels embracing this agenda. Will this nation's leadership be strong enough to stand up to the woke nonsense? At present, it does not look encouraging. Until strong leadership emerges, perhaps we should start with ourselves. I said at the beginning of this chapter that I hope it can at least help you feel comfortable voicing your opinion on Aboriginal affairs. If you feel you can do that then I will have succeeded. If I haven't, then I am open to your feedback—and I promise I won't take offence.

Dr Anthony Dillon is an academic and commentator on Indigenous affairs. He believes that the current popular ideologies which portray Indigenous people merely as victims of history and White Australia (the invasion and racism) are doing as much damage to Aboriginal people as drugs and alcohol. He strongly believes that the only way we will 'Close the Gap' between disadvantaged Indigenous Australians and the rest of the population is by ensuring that all Indigenous people have access to the opportunities that most Australians take for granted. His writings can be found at www.anthonydillon.com.au.

GENDER FLUID LAWS: CANCELLING SEX, WOMEN, PARENTAL RIGHTS AND THREATENING DEMOCRACY

PATRICK BYRNE

Two world views collide

As a result of radical transgender theory, biological girls and women are now required to compete against biological boys and men who identify as female playing in many female sports.

In 2019, Australia's Coalition of Major Professional and Participation Sports (COMPPS) and the Australian Human Rights Commission released *Guidelines for the inclusion of transgender and gender diverse people in sport. The guidelines* say biological males have only to self-identify as female to participate, except in the elite competition, where they are required to reduce their testosterone below a prescribed level for a year.

COMPPS represents all football codes, cricket, netball and tennis, covering 16,000 clubs with nine million participants.

While COMPPS say the *guidelines* focus on inclusion in community sport, they also apply to amateur and professional state, national and international competitions. They ignore the reality that having more muscle, greater bone strength and weight are important, particularly in contact sports where the disparity between biologically defined male and female competitors is a crucial factor in deciding who wins and who loses.

In campaigning for women's only sports, Tasmanian Senator Claire Chandler says she has been contacted by hundreds of sporting women who are concerned about the erosion of female-only competition but fear the consequences of speaking out. 'I've heard horrific stories of women being threatened, suspended and told their common-sense views are in breach of the law', she told *The Australian* (2 October 2020).

In 2016, the Federal government announced there would be no new funding to the controversial Safe Schools Australia transgender sex-education program in schools. The program heavily promoted the contested idea of gender fluidity to children and teenagers. It was marketed as an anti-bullying program but it is recorded in Victoria's Parliamentary Hansard (26 October 2016) that Roz Ward, one of its founders, openly said at a 2014 Safe Schools National Symposium the program is 'not about celebrating diversity; not about stopping bullying. [It's] about gender and sexual diversity'.

Ward, who is a member of the radical Socialist Alternative activist group, also argues 'Marxism offers both the hope and the strategy needed to create a world where human sexuality, gender and how we relate to our bodies can blossom in extraordinary new and amazing ways that we can only try to imagine today'.

Despite the Federal government's announcement, many education departments across the nation continue to include gender fluidity in the curriculum and have programs to support children transitioning to another sex/gender. This includes boys who identify as girls being able to access girls' sport and safe spaces. Education authorities claim that these policies are required of state schools by federal, state and territory anti-discrimination laws.

Gender fluidity, better described as the ideology of transgenderism, is a highly contested 'belief' from the social sciences that conflicts with biological science and the lived experience of the vast majority of people. In a survey carried out by academics Anthony Smith and Paul Badcock at La Trobe University's Australian Research Centre in Sex,

Health and Society 97.4 per cent of men and 97.7 per cent of women interviewed were happy to identify as heterosexual.

Gender identity laws are imposing on state, private and religious institutions, under threat of legal penalties, a belief that human sexual identity is diverse and fluid.

It is cancelling the sex-based rights of women to their own sports, safe spaces, schools, clubs, language and their identity as being female. It is cancelling parental rights to raise their children as they see fit, while puberty blockers carry many known and unknown medical risks for children medically changing their sex.

Moreover, the imposition of legal penalties for noncompliance threatens freedom of conscience and speech, a necessary cornerstone for a tolerant Australian democracy.

Gender fluid theory

The Western world is witnessing an extraordinary contest of ideas between the evidence-based, scientific and common-sense apprehension of reality that human beings are biologically male or female, and the transgender 'belief' from the social sciences that a person can have a gender identity separate from, or in place of, her or his sex recorded at birth.

The biological world view recognises that a person's sex is part of his or her inherent, immutable, biological hardware. Sex is defined not just by males having XY chromosomes and females XX chromosomes, but in the end by reproductive function. Only a biological male can impregnate a female and only a biological female can become pregnant and bear a child. The terms man, woman and sex have been self-evident facts that did not require definitions in law.

Based on a person's sex being self-evident at birth, a wide range of laws (like birth registration, marriage and anti-discriminant laws), regulations, codes of conduct and cultural practices have recognised each person as having many sex-based rights, protections, privileges and access to services. These include determining access to schools, sports competitions and private safe places, provision of medical services and housing prisoners.

In opposition to the biological world view, the gender fluid, or transgender, world view is a sociological theory, a belief that a person can self-identify and have a gender identity different from their birth sex. Gender identity is said to be wholly a social construct that is subjectively defined by a person's cultural and social software.

Transgenderism arose out of currents from the Sexual Revolution. In 1965, Psychologist and sexologist John Money founded the Johns Hopkins University Gender Identity Clinic in Baltimore, USA. He was one of the first theorists to promote the idea of socially constructed gender. Although he encouraged sex-reassignment surgery, Johns Hopkins discontinued transitioning surgery in the 1970s after it was demonstrated that the practice brought no important benefits. (The Public Discourse, 10 June 2015)

In sociology, post-modernist queer theory embraced transgenderism on the assertion of French Philosopher Michel Foucault's 1971 essay 'Nietzsche, Genealogy, History', that 'nothing in man—not even his body—is sufficiently stable to serve as the basis for self-recognition or for understanding other men'. Queer theory stands in opposition to all that is normal, being 'outside the bounds of normal society'. It embraces transgenderism for 'breaking the rules for sex and gender' with no defined limits.

Gayle Rubin, a cultural anthropologist who is an activist and theorist of sex and gender politics, wrote the founding document of queer theory, *Thinking Sex: Notes for a Radical Theory of the Politics of Sexuality* (1984), while Judith Butler has become its most celebrated advocate in Western universities.

Queer theory fails to grasp the disturbing consequences of Foucault's assertion: if no man is like any other man, then there is no common human nature, therefore there are no universal human rights. Foucault cancels universal human rights, reopening the possibility that some of us are more equal than others.

How many people identify as transgender? A 2016 study by the

University of California's Williams Institute on Sexual Orientation and Gender Identity Law and Public Policy claims 0.6 per cent of Americans are transgender. However, the study's broad definition of transgender is itself fluid—experiencing a different gender identity, feeling you are a different person, a change in physical appearance, as well as having undergone surgical and medical transitioning treatments. Hence the 0.6 per cent figure is problematic.

The corollary of the Williams Institute study is that at least 99.4 per cent of people identify with their birth sex. That includes gays, lesbians, bisexuals and heterosexuals.

Disregarding this reality, the Australian Federal Attorney-General's Department adopted the transgender world view when it issued the 2013 *Australian Government Guidelines on the Recognition of Sex and Gender*, saying that a person's gender identity is defined by their 'outward social markers, including their name, outward appearance, mannerism and dress', that is, via factors that are all determined by how they feel.

Such a definition is ambiguous. Does being a boy mean behaving in the ways boys typically behave: engaging in rough-and-tumble play and expressing an interest in sports and liking toy guns more than dolls? Conversely, does this mean that a boy who plays with dolls, hates guns, and refrains from sports or rough-and-tumble play might be considered to be a girl, rather than simply a boy who represents an exception to the typical patterns of male behaviour? Are such behaviours just personality traits rather than descriptions of sexual identify?

Despite such ambiguity, the gender fluid world view advocates four concepts.

First, the concept of a person's gender identity being defined by how they feel opens an unlimited number of ways a person can identify and claim legally created gender identity rights:

- a biological man can identify as a woman, and a biological woman can identify as a man,
- a person can be at any point on a spectrum of anywhere between 100 per cent male and 100 per cent female,

- a person can reject the idea of male and female altogether and identify with a gender term like androgynous, or gender queer, or any of a host of other non-binary terms, and
- a person can identify as having no gender, i.e. as being genderless.

These forms of gender identity raise many questions.

Conceptually, how can a person be on a spectrum from male to female unless there are first biological males and females? How can a person be non-binary (not one of two sexes) if there are not first two biological sexes? How can a person be genderless unless there are first two genders/sexes? As trans means to change, how can a person change (trans) to something other than their sex, unless they first have a sex?

There is a further anthropological question: if a person's sex is fluid and changeable, can a person also change their age, their race or their species?

Second, gender fluid theory opposes what it condemns as heteronormativity, the theory that children are conditioned from the day they are born into believing that they are a boy or a girl by how they are recorded on their birth certificate, the blue or pink clothes they wear, the toys they are given to play with, the schools they attend, etc.

In opposition to heteronormativity, gender fluid theory advocates comprehensive change in every legal and cultural aspect of a person's life to a transgender, or fluid gender world view. Hence, the importance the theory places on changing laws, codes of conduct and, most importantly, introducing gender fluid sex-education programs into schools regardless of protests by students, parents and teachers.

Third, it advocates child agency: the idea that a child is just a small adult who is capable of acting independently and making decisions around issues such as gender identity, particularly once they have been educated into the idea that sex and gender identity are fluid. However, if children are just small adults capable of making decisions about sexual identity, can they also join the army, marry as children and have sex, be given a driver's licence and legally consume alcohol? The whole idea of child agency trashes an entire discipline: child psychology. Child psychology is reduced to being psychology of small adults.

Fourth, advocacy for political change to recognise the transgender world view in law and culture morphs gender fluid sociological theory into a political agenda directed at legally recognising the transgender world view in laws, codes and culture.

As it advances in all these areas, the fluid gender world view comes into inevitable conflict with what biology says about sex, creating wide and deep political, legal, educational and cultural contradictions and conflicts.

Biological sex versus gender fluid

Doctors Lawrence Meyer and Paul McHugh, in a landmark review of 'Sexuality and Gender: Findings from the Biological, Psychological, and Social Sciences' (*The New Atlantis*, No. 50, 2016), say: 'The only variable that serves as the fundamental and reliable basis for biologists to distinguish the sexes of animals is their role in reproduction, not some other behavioural or biological trait'.

The extent of these biological differences is profound. From 550 adult donors in 2017, researchers at the Weizmann Institute of Science, one of the world's leading multidisciplinary basic research institutions in the natural and exact sciences, examined the 20,000 protein-coding genes in human DNA to find differences in expression in each tissue according to a person's sex. They identified around '6,500 genes with activity that was biased toward one sex or the other in at least one tissue'. (Weizmann Institute of Science, 7 May 2017)

The study found '[g]ene expression for muscle building was higher in men; that for fat storage was higher in women'. Another 'gene expression in the liver in women that regulates drug metabolism, provid[es] molecular evidence for the known difference in drug processing between women and men'. Diseases and conditions to which people are more prone according to their biological sex were identified.

The Weizmann report indicates that the biological hardware differences between men and women are far more extensive than had previously been understood. To that end, the US National Academy of

Medicine's Committee on Understanding the Biology of Sex and Gender Differences has created a whole new branch of science known as 'sex-based biology'. (*Pharmacy Practice*, Granada, 2016 Jan-Mar; 14(1): 708)

Co-opting intersex

Not only does gender fluid theory ignore such biological evidence of the inherent nature of biological sex but it also misappropriates the condition known as intersex, or disorders of sexual development, as evidence that people can be other than male or female.

Typically, gender fluid theory says that intersex refers to a very small group of the population who are neither fully male nor fully female, opening the possibility of a third sex/gender or many sexes/genders.

The first problem is that you cannot first define gender identity as a social construct based on feelings and then claim intersex, which is identified on a biological basis, as evidence of a third and hence a spectrum of sexes/genders. Which is it?

Second, the Intersex Society of North America (ISNA) insists that intersex is a disorder of sexual development and is not evidence of a third sex or gender. It also prefers the term 'disorder of sexual development' in place of 'intersex', which can imply that a person can be other than male or female.

Feminist political philosopher Rebecca Reilly-Cooper has pointed out that, as a disorder of sexual development, intersex is no more evidence that humans are other than male or female any more than a person born without legs could be used to claim that humans can be other than bipedal, that is, stand upright on two legs.

Indeed, ISNA says that research shows that the vast majority of intersex people identify with their sex as recorded at birth, contrary to what is implied by advocates of gender fluidity.

A philosophical interrogation

On what basis does a gender fluid ideology claim to override inherent biological sex?

The ancient Greek philosophers would have understood today's conflict of world views. Greek dualists believed the mind and body were separate entities and that the mind could dominate the body. Similarly, fluid gender theory argues the mind can control the body to such a degree that if a male identifies as female he becomes female.

In opposition to the dualist view were philosophers like Aristotle. He argued although we speak of the mind and body differently, they are an integrated whole just as 'the wax [of a candle] and its shape are one'. Hence, it is normal (in accordance with its nature) for the mind to see the body's sex as an inherent aspect of the person.

The philosophical issue has consequences.

If Aristotle is correct, the mind of a biological male who identifies as female is in conflict with the reality of the person's body, in a similar way that an anorexic female's perception of her body as obese is in conflict with the realty of her being slim and undernourished. If fluid gender theorists demand that a person with gender dysphoria be affirmed in their chosen identity, will they also insist on supporting a person with anorexia nervosa to continue denying themselves food until death?

Equally, if the spate of laws being introduced across Australia to prohibit conversion therapy prioritise the mind over the body in cases of gender dysphoria, should not laws also prioritise the mind over the body in anorexia cases?

Gender identity laws

Led by federal, state and territory human-rights commissions, governments have introduced gender-identity laws, regulations and public-service guidelines with very little political opposition. In addition to these laws redefining human sexual identity they are also cancelling inherent sex-based rights.

These changes have included:
- Federal, state and territory anti-discrimination laws redefining the identity of the human person by making gender identity and

sexual/gender orientation protected attributes, accompanied
with penalties for those discriminating against a person based on
these protected attributes,

- The Federal Marriage Act 1961 being changed in 2017 to
recognise marriage between any two people according to
their fluid gender identity (transgender marriage), or by their
biological sex (heterosexual and same-sex marriage),

- State and territory births, deaths and marriage registration acts
being changed to allow recognition of a person by their sex
or their gender identity (for example, the Australian Capital
Territory birth registration forms recognise a person as Male,
Female, Indeterminate, Unspecified or Intersex), and to allow a
person to change their sex/gender identity according to how they
feel, and

- States and territories introducing laws to ban conversion
practices, that is, laws prohibiting any counselling and
treatments that do not affirm a person in their self-chosen
gender identity.

One of the most significant changes was made in 2013 when,
under then Labor Attorney-General Mark Dreyfus, the federal Sex
Discrimination Act (SDA) was amended to give protected attribute
status to a person's 'gender identity'. Immediately afterwards, the
Attorney-General's Department issued the *Australian Government
Guidelines on the Recognition of Sex and Gender* (2013, updated
2015), which required the sex identifier to record a person as Male,
Female, Indeterminate, Unspecified or Intersex on all official federal
government forms, including passports.

Both commonwealth and similar state and territory laws have played
and are continuing to play a key role in driving gender fluid cancel
culture in schools and sport.

Schools complying with gender fluidity

The 2013 gender identity protections introduced into the Sex
Discrimination Act (SDA) became a key driver of gender fluidity

programs and policies in Australia's state schools. The SDA (Section 21) says government schools cannot discriminate against a student based on his or her gender identity or sexual orientation, by 'refusing or failing to accept the person's application for admission' or by 'denying the student, or limiting the student's access, to any benefit' the school provides, or by 'expelling' or 'subjecting the student to any other detriment'.

Only weeks after the gender identity provisions were inserted into the SDA the federal Labor government granted $8 million for the controversial Safe Schools Program to be rolled out across Australia. The program was developed in Victoria by La Trobe University's Australian Research Centre in Sex, Health and Society and as previously mentioned involved the activist Roz Ward.

In 2016, following an inquiry by the subsequent Liberal administration, the government announced that there would be no new funding for the program. However, the federal government's Student Wellbeing Hub continues to provide considerable Safe Schools resources including a guide for schools on students transitioning titled the *All Of US* years 7 and 8 resource on gender diversity and sexual diversity, as well as numerous videos. Other states have rebadged Safe Schools resources for their schools or adopted similar programs. Only NSW has taken steps to stop the teaching of gender fluidity in schools.

To comply with the amended SDA and various state and territory anti-discrimination laws at least four state education departments (NSW, Victoria, Queensland and South Australia) have issued policies requiring state school authorities to support a biological boy who self-identifies as a girl to access girls' toilets, showers, change rooms, sports, camps and dormitories.

These policies expose how problematic the entire issue is. For example, the NSW Department of Education and Communities Legal Issues Bulletin No 55 (December 2014) assessed the risks for 'use of toilet and change rooms' as 'high', suggesting that other students face not just 'discomfort' but potentially more serious issues. Risk management involves: 'Doors provided to change room cubicles of their identified gender. Student must change in a cubicle. Staff to monitor length of time in change room. Staff and student to report any incidents in the change room to Principal ... Zero tolerance to "skylarking" in change rooms'.

Are teachers to be rostered outside toilets? What happens to a male teacher's reputation if he finds it necessary to intervene in a female toilet, shower or change room? These requirements come at a time when there is serious community concern over child-on-child sexual abuse in schools.

The South Australian policy goes further. It warns principals and teachers that '[f]ailure to provide transgender students with access to appropriate toilet and change facilities may breach anti-discrimination legislation'. Presumably, this means that school authorities could face legal penalties for non-compliance with these policies, and face disciplinary action, loss of professional qualifications and employment.

Parental 'lockout'

Parents are also being marginalised and cancelled by the SDA operating in conjunction with an interpretation of case law. The UK's Gillick case (1985) effectively ruled, while children can be guided by their parents a child has a right to autonomy which develops gradually as it grows and develops their capacity for making decisions. This is the concept of the 'mature minor'. The case has been recognised in Australian jurisprudence.

Still being promoted by federal and some state governments, the Safe Schools *Guide to Supporting a Student to Affirm or Transition Gender Identity at School* advances the Gillick principle. It invokes both the SDA and Gillick principle to encourage teachers to allow students to change their gender without parental approval. It says about gender transitioning: 'It may be possible to consider a student a mature minor and able to make decisions without parental consent'.

What of the right of parents to expect a high-level duty of care for their children and of their 'prior right to choose the kind of education that shall be given to their children', as recognised in Article 26 (c) of the Universal Declaration of Human Rights?

What of the right of other students to privacy in toilets, showers and change rooms? What of the right of girls to fair play in sports?

Currently, the SDA provisions apply only to state schools. However, the Morrison Liberal Government has asked the Australian Law Reform Commission to investigate limiting or removing exemptions for faith-based schools and institutions. If that happens, state education gender fluid policies would likely be forced on faith-based schools, thereby cancelling religious beliefs about the binary nature of sex. And there is the danger religious schools would be forced to employ teachers who actively promote transgenderism.

Sports complying with gender fluidity

The 2019 transgender inclusionary policies of the Coalition of Major Professional and Participation Sports (COMPPS) is a prime example of how gender fluid ideology is being adopted in sporting and corporate codes of conduct. These policies are cancelling the inherent right of biological women to fair play in their own sports.

Rugby Australia (RA) demonstrates not only the broad application of this policy, but also how the sport is now deeply divided over the issue.

Well before the COMPPS *Guidelines for the inclusion of transgender and gender diverse people in sport,* RA had established its *Gender Identity Dispensation Procedure*, which effectively requires women and girls to accept males who identify as female in the female competition. Self-identification is the only criterion for being accepted as female, except at the elite level, where transgender players are required to lower their testosterone levels.

Furthermore, RA's *Code of Conduct* not only covers professional players, but coaches, administrators, officers of a rugby body, match officials, spectators/parents, fans and all other participants. It says all involved in the sport must treat 'everyone equally regardless of gender or gender identity, sexual orientation, ethnicity' etc., and must 'not use social media as a means to breach any of the [*Code's*] expectations and requirements' to bring the sport into 'disrepute or discredit'.

Whereas the star Australian rugby player Israel Folau was sacked by rugby authorities for expressing a moral opinion about gays and lesbians under the current RA *Code*, should female players, parents or fans oppose a transgender male-to-female playing in the female competition, they are held to be effectively calling for that player to be excluded from the female sport. In doing so, they could be accused of discrimination and, therefore, of bringing the sport into greater 'disrepute or discredit' than Folau.

Penalties for breaches of the *Code* are proportionate to the offence, the most serious leading to 'suspension for a specified number of matches or period of time' and 'withdrawal of … membership', that is, expulsion from the game, as happened with Folau. Parents and fans can face 'exclusion orders' from rugby playing grounds.

RA teamed up with the COMPPS trans-inclusionary drive shortly before World Rugby went in the opposite direction with its *Transgender Guideline* (October 2020) which bans biological males who identify as female from playing in the women's rugby international competition, except in non-contact games. The policy is not binding on national leagues.

World Rugby's FAQ on the new policy says that research has shown that biological males are stronger by 25 to 50 per cent, more powerful by 30 per cent, 40 per cent heavier, about 15 per cent faster than biological females, and have 160 per cent higher punching power.

It says: 'The separation of athletes into two categories therefore creates meaning in the outcomes for both categories, by removing the significant effect of testosterone's effects on the outcome. For contact and combat sports, this separation also reduces the safety risk, because the outcomes of testosterone's effects—size, speed, muscle mass, strength and power—are significant risk factors for injury, and so an acceptable level of safety of those who are "disadvantaged" can only be achieved if the effects of those androgens are removed from the risk analysis by separation into two categories'.

The division now between World Rugby and Rugby Australia is yet to be played out. It is also yet to be played out in many other sports.

Whereas the Sex Discrimination Act was originally designed to protect the inherent sex-based rights of biological women, it now supports granting the same rights to biological males who identify as women, with no direction on how to resolve resultant conflicts between newly created transgender rights and inherent sex-based rights.

Deep and wide legal and cultural dilemmas

The biological world view and the gender fluid world view of human sexuality are inherently contradictory and cannot be resolved to the satisfaction of both world views. The conflicts occur in all places where sex-based rights apply.

For example:

- Are women's-only services (for example, hair and waxing salons), domestic violence shelters, gyms, sessions in swimming pools, and many other female privileges and services also to be made available to any biological male who identifies as a woman?
- How are medical professionals to administer appropriate sex-specific medications and treatments if it is unclear whether a patient is biologically male or biologically female?
- How can researchers successfully undertake clinical trials of new drugs and medical procedures that depend on knowing whether a person is female or male, if sexuality is fluid and indeterminate?
- Should violent rapists who were born male, but who now identify as female, be accommodated in women's prisons?
- In a workplace that invokes the SDA to impose gender-neutral language on staff, will a man married to a woman be required to refer to her only as his 'partner' so as not to offend transgenders? Will he face social sanctions or refusal of new employment contracts if he fails to use gender-neutral language to describe his wife, son, daughter, friends and work colleagues?
- Can a biological male who identifies as female claim benefits reserved for biological women in affirmative action programs?

In 2018, more than 300 women quit the UK Labour Party over a decision to include men who self-identify as female as candidates on the party's all-women shortlists that are used to select candidates, from parliamentary elections down to local government.

Not surprisingly, many feminists strongly oppose gender-identity laws for cancelling hard-won women's rights. These include veteran feminists like Australian writer and public intellectual Germaine Greer and American Camille Paglia, professor at the University of the Arts in Philadelphia. Harry Potter author J.K. Rowling has also taken a strong stand against transgenderism cancelling the sex-based rights of women. The world-famous tennis player Martina Navratilova (who identifies as a lesbian and socially progressive) has also earned the ire of gender activists by arguing there is no place for men who have transitioned in women's tennis.

Gender fluid ideology weaponises the power of the state and the courts to force its world view on everyone and to silence those who hold to the biological world view under threat of penalties that include loss of jobs.

Towards an authoritarian state?

Legal protections for gender identity are far more powerful weapons against what the vast majority of people regard as normal sexuality and family, against people of faith and against secular people who hold the biological world view, than legal protections for sexual orientation. For example, gay males play in male sports, but males who identify as female can seek to play in female sports and use female toilets, showers, change rooms, dormitories, etc.

When laws make a person's gender identity a protected attribute they cancel the sex-based rights, privileges, protections and access to services of more than 99.4 per cent of people who recognise their sex as inherent. This creates deep conflicts across wide areas of law, workplaces, education, medicine, sport, provision of service, social clubs, and many other areas.

This is analogous to the state making Catholic beliefs a protected attribute in anti-discrimination law. That would mean that state schools would be forced to teach the Catholic faith and atheist organisations would be forced to employ Catholics. Effectively, the government would impose Catholicism as a state religion intolerant of other people who hold any other belief. This would mark a shift from a tolerant, neutral democracy to an authoritarian state imposing one belief on all citizens.

Gender identity laws have a targeted purpose. What Brendan O'Neill, the London-based editor of *Spiked* magazine, attributed to the gay agenda more appropriately describes the hostile ideological agenda of transgenderism. He said it is fundamentally hostile 'to the straight world—which means not just people who are sexually straight, but also so-called straight culture and straight values, straightlacedness itself, ways of life that are based on commitment, privacy, familial sovereignty, things that tend to be viewed by the modern cultural clerisy as outdated or, worse, dangerous and destructive'.

It is 'fundamentally about eradicating old moral values and enforcing new ones … [I]t constantly verges on being coercive, expressing a hostility towards its opponents that tends to treat them, not simply as wrong or pesky, but as actual blocks, as "ideological enemies" to the elite's attempted enforcement of a new moral outlook'. (*Spiked*, 30 April 2014)

Gender identity laws enforcing this 'new moral outlook' sets a tolerant democracy, where all beliefs and faiths are tolerated in the public square, on the road to becoming an authoritarian state.

A way ahead

Despite the raft of gender identity laws now imposing the gender fluid world view on society there is a way to restore protections of sex-based rights.

Biological sex is self-evident in utero, at birth and throughout a person's life. The vast majority of people recognise their biological sex as inherent, whereas only a small minority identify as transgender. So, logically, the biological world view should be recognised in law by putting the biological definitions of 'man', 'woman' and 'sex' into relevant laws.

Such legal recognition of the biological world view and the rights that naturally flow from biological sex protects the inherent rights of the vast majority. It provides certainty in law while still allowing cultural recognition of those who identify as transgender, preserving their liberty (freedom without political interference) to change their sex or gender. If it doesn't impose restrictions, it preserves liberty and freedoms and allows for diversity.

Everyone, including transgenders, are protected by defamation laws, anti-vilification laws, employment laws, etc. Effective anti-bullying policies and education programs teach people not to bully anyone and to respect all people.

There is a final paradox with gender fluid ideology.

Imposing gender neutral language, toilets, showers, change rooms and sports are supposed to be examples of sexual 'diversity'. In reality this makes everyone uniform, same-same, one shade of grey. This is the opposite of diversity.

Gender fluid ideology cancels what our eyes, evidence-based biological science and anthropology tell us are the different, complementary male and female sexes. Writing the biological definitions of 'man', 'woman' and 'sex' into law would protect biological diversity and the lived experience of the vast majority of humanity throughout history. Vive la *difference*!

Patrick J Byrne BA, BTheol., is President of the National Civic Council, founded by the late BA Santamaria in 1941. He has been a long-time contributor to the NCC's News Weekly magazine on social, economic, political and international issues. He is author of Transgender: One Shade of Grey *(2018) and a short book on this issue,* The Little Grey Book on Sex and Transgender *(2019).*

THE PAST IS THE KEY TO THE PRESENT

IAN PLIMER

Since planet Earth formed 4,567 million years ago, climate has always changed. Major terrestrial and extra-terrestrial processes have always driven climate change. Past climate changes have been greater and faster than anything measured today. The Sun has driven past climate changes and there is no evidence to suggest that the present is different from the past. As in the past, water vapour is the main greenhouse gas in the atmosphere. However, for the last 30 years we have been told that humans drive climate change and unless carbon dioxide emissions are greatly reduced then the planet is doomed. Did anyone notice a change in major planetary processes?

The Sun emits variable amounts of energy, the distance between the Earth and the Sun changes, the magnetic shielding from solar energy varies and changes to the shape of the continents and oceans modifies surface heat distribution. Planet Earth is dynamic and the concept that humans drive climate change infers the planet was static until we sinful Western humans started to emit carbon dioxide from industry.

Planet Earth has had three atmospheres. The primordial atmosphere comprised methane, ammonia, water vapour, carbon dioxide and noble gases. Because such gases are found in space and on other planets, the primordial atmosphere may have been part of the original cosmos. Nitrogen compounds in this early atmosphere decomposed to nitrogen gas and hydrogen, which escaped back to space. As soon as there was surface water on Earth, there was bacterial life.

Colonies of bacterial life formed reefs in shallow warm waters about 3,700 million years ago. These reefs are well preserved in the Pilbara (WA). Over the long history of time, reefs and numerous past great barrier reefs have died due to exposure when sea level fell during glacial times and thrived in warm shallow waters when sea level was high. Disease and sediment inundation have also killed reefs. Primordial hydrogen, noble gases, carbon dioxide, sulphur gases, methane and water vapour are still leaking up ocean floor fractures and from volcanoes into the atmosphere. Hydrogen continues to escape from planet Earth into space. In the primordial atmosphere, sulphides and uranium minerals existed in surface water without oxidising showing that there was almost no oxygen in the atmosphere.

During the Huronian Glaciation at about 2,500 million years ago, the planet was a snowball with ice at sea level at the equator. There were numerous periods when ice expanded and contracted. Meltwaters flushed a huge volume of nutrients into the seas. As a result, bacterial life exploded and evolved into oxygen-emitting bacteria that conducted genocide against the original anaerobic bacteria on Earth. Refugees of this genocide still exist in bogs, deep in the Earth's crust and even in our stomach. The atmosphere started to accumulate oxygen, soils rusted from green to red-brown colour, the oceans rusted and massive amounts of iron ore was precipitated onto the sea floor. The Huronian shows that rocks, life, the atmosphere and oceans interact. They still do today.

In Earth's middle age, the atmosphere had up to hundreds of times more carbon dioxide than at present. The carbon dioxide was naturally sequestered into huge volumes of marine dolomite sediments which contain 48 per cent carbon dioxide by weight. Experimental mineralogy shows that dolomite (calcium magnesium carbonate) can only precipitate when there is an atmosphere of at least 10 per cent carbon dioxide. At present, the Earth's atmosphere contains 0.04 per cent carbon dioxide. Henry's Law shows that atmospheric carbon dioxide is in equilibrium with ocean water and there is an exchange of carbon dioxide between the oceans and the atmosphere. Over time, emissions of carbon dioxide do not accumulate in the atmosphere as there is a constant sequestering of carbon dioxide into sediments and life. In the Earth's middle age, stromatolitic life also sequestered carbon dioxide and bacteria continued to add oxygen to the atmosphere.

The third atmosphere was during the last 20 per cent of time when there was an explosion of animal and plant life on Earth. The Earth's atmosphere increased in oxygen to almost its current level (21 per cent). At times the global oxygen content was up to 35 per cent which facilitated global forest fires and increased erosion. Atmospheric oxygen derives from life. Oxygen is not a primordial gas, it does not leak from the planet, does not occur in space and is not part of magmatic fluids exhaled from deep in the Earth via volcanoes. If oxygen is detected by spectral measurement of the atmospheres of extra-solar system planets, then there is life elsewhere in the Universe.

Over the last half billion years, carbon dioxide has been decreasing because of sequestering into marine limestone (calcium carbonate), shells, algae and muds and terrestrial plants and coals. At present, the Earth's atmospheric carbon dioxide content is historically low. If halved, there would be no life on Earth. Again, this sequestration process is controlled by Henry's Law which regulates equilibrium between carbon dioxide in the atmosphere and dissolved carbon dioxide in seawater.

For thousands of millions of years, carbon dioxide in seawater occurs as dissolved gas, bicarbonate ions and carbonate ions. These ions control the pH of the oceans and, because calcium ions are continually added to seawater by rivers and combine with carbonate to precipitate calcium carbonate (limestone), carbon dioxide is constantly removed from sea water. This process of buffering prevents oceans becoming acid over time. Seawater is also buffered by circulation through the top 5km of the oceanic crust and, during circulation, reacts with seafloor sediments and ocean floor volcanic basalts. Throughout most of time, the oceans have been alkaline and the geological past and geochemistry show that a slight increase in a trace gas in the atmosphere makes no difference to ocean alkalinity.

There have been six major ice ages all of which had multiple glaciations when ice sheets expanded and multiple interglacials when ice sheets contracted. All these ice ages were initiated when the atmospheric carbon dioxide content was higher than now and during the most intense ice age, the atmospheric carbon dioxide content was at least hundreds of times higher than at present and sea level rose and fell by 1.5km.

The past shows that carbon dioxide was a major atmospheric gas whereas now it is a trace gas and yet we are expected to believe that adding minute amounts of a trace gas to the atmosphere will change planetary systems that have operated for thousands of millions of years. In times past when there was a high atmospheric carbon dioxide, there was no runaway global warming and there were cyclical glaciations and interglacials. If global warming did not occur in the past with a high carbon dioxide atmosphere, there is no reason why carbon dioxide-driven global warming should occur now.

During the Earth's middle age in a time known as the Cryogenian, glaciation occurred between 715 and 660 million years ago (Sturtian glaciation). Ice sheets were at sea level, at the Equator and covered the planet. Sea level was some 1.5km lower and the atmosphere had a high carbon dioxide content. Five pulses of the Sturtian glaciation have been recognised during which times global ice sheets expanded and contracted. Bacterial life survived during these gruelling times. The Sturtian glaciation ended suddenly, sea level and atmospheric temperature rose, shallow warm waters covered the continental shelves and nutrients were added to the oceans by meltwaters.

There have been reefs in shallow warm waters on planet Earth for the last 3,700 million years. Up until 660 million years ago, these reefs contained only single-celled organisms that precipitated dolomite. Immediately after the Sturtian glaciation, reefs with multicellular life appeared between 660 and 650 million years ago and this evolutionary diversification was probably driven by the addition of nutrients into the oceans at the end of the Sturtian glaciation. These multicellular fossils and possibly corals were first found in the Arkaroola Reef in the far North Flinders Ranges (SA).

The planet cooled again during the Marinoan glaciation between 650 and 635 million years ago. The Arkaroola Reef was left high and dry and died. The first multicellular life became extinct and this trial-and-error experiment to form multicellular life failed. Modern exposed limestone reefs also die, this is happening in some places in the Great Barrier Reef as the land has risen more than a metre over the last 5,000 years. In the Marinoan, the planet had ice at sea level, at the equator and was covered with ice.

After the Marinoan, sea level and temperature rose, sea ice broke up and dropped boulders onto the sea floor, iron ores precipitated and warm shallow waters covered the continental shelves. Again, bacterial life survived these long cold times and evolved into multicellular life called the Ediacaran fauna just after the oceans were swamped with nutrients carried by meltwaters. The Ediacaran was first discovered in the North Flinders Ranges. This time, the evolutionary experiment to form multicellular life succeeded because after the Marinoan there was a long warm period. There was an explosion of life, the soft-bodied Ediacaran became food for armoured predators, major main groups of life appeared and sequestered even more carbon dioxide into shells and limestone reefs.

Past climate changes have been driven by tectonic cycles every 400 million years that changed the shape of continents and oceans. For example, the joining of North America to South America by volcanic rocks some 2.67 million years ago prevented the mixing of Atlantic and Pacific waters, changed the surface heat balance and produced a sudden cooling during which time our genus Homo appeared. The same tectonic processes are taking place at present.

Sedimentary rocks are subducted and sequestered deep under continents, these rocks are heated under pressure and leak carbon dioxide, methane and other gases into the atmosphere and hot springs. The pulling apart of the oceans at mid ocean ridges releases heat and carbon dioxide into the bottom waters. This carbon dioxide is dissolved in the deep high-pressure saline bottom waters and is released into the atmosphere thousands of years later during oceanic upwelling when water salinity and pressure decrease and temperature increases. The heated ocean water at the mid ocean ridges changes oceanic circulation and there is strong volcanological evidence that the modern El Niño-La Niña cycle and blobs of warm ocean water derive from heat exchange from new volcanic rocks.

Every 143 million years, the Solar System has a bad galactic address and the Earth undergoes increased bombardment by cosmic radiation. The terrestrial and solar magnetic fields protect Earth from solar and cosmic radiation. However, during times when the solar magnetic field is reduced (e.g. when there are no sunspots) or increased cosmic radiation (e.g. during supernoval explosions), the Earth is bombarded by more cosmic radiation. More clouds form, less solar radiation reaches the Earth's surface and the planet cools. This process has been validated with theoretical and experimental studies and measurement of cosmogenic isotopic fingerprints from past supernoval explosions. Over the last 1,000 years, historical high cosmic radiation bombardment is correlated with past reduced sunspot activity and global coolings with the resultant famines, disease pandemics, increased warfare and depopulation.

Changes in the Earth's orbit from elliptical to circular has 100,000-year cycles derives from a combination of 95,000- and 125,000-year cycles due to the gravitational pull of the large outer planets. The axis of the Earth's rotation changes every 41,000 years which also changes the distance of the Earth from the Sun as does the wobbling of the Earth on 23,000-year cycles.

Polar ice has only existed on Earth for less than 20 per cent of time and we are currently in an ice age that started 34 million years ago when South America separated from Antarctica thereby thermally isolating Antarctica by circum-polar ocean currents. During the current ice age, there have been orbitally-driven cyclical glaciations and interglacials and the last few of these are preserved as chemical fingerprints in the Greenland and Antarctic ice sheets. The Earth is currently towards the end of an orbitally-driven interglacial that peaked about 6,000 years ago when global temperature and sea level were higher than at present.

Less well known are the changes in the energy emitted from the Sun every 10,000, 1,500, 217 and 87 years. Better known are the 11-year solar cycles that have been measured for 350 years. Periods such as the Minoan Warming, Roman Warming, Dark Ages, Medieval Warming, Little Ice Age and the Modern Warming are well recorded in history and chemical fingerprints show an origin based on changes in solar radiation. History shows that the best times to be a human on Earth are in warm periods, like now, when population and economic prosperity increased, whereas in cold times death, depopulation, plagues, war and starvation were predominant. Over geological time, life struggled in cold times and thrived in warm times.

Oceanic decadal oscillations and lunar tidal cycles are on 60-year and 11-year cycles respectively. Ancient Chinese calendars are based on the 60-year Pacific Decadal Oscillation. Non-cyclical asteroid impacts and supervolcanoes also change climate by filling the atmosphere with dust and sulphurous aerosols which block solar radiation. No large past climate changes can be attributed to atmospheric carbon dioxide changes.

There have been five major mass extinctions and more than 20 minor mass extinctions since complex multicellular life appeared on Earth. At least 20 per cent of multicellular species disappear in a minor mass extinction and at least 50 per cent of multicellular species disappeared during the major mass extinctions at 440, 365, 250, 210 and 65 million years ago, mainly due to volcanoes and asteroid impacts. No past minor or major mass extinction has been due to slight warming or a barely measurable increase in atmospheric carbon dioxide and we are not in a period of mass extinction. Loss of individual species by extinction is part of the normal constant species turnover. Since multicellular life appeared on Earth, the number of species on Earth has increased at a rate greater than species loss.

At present, there is a turnover of species with species extinction concurrent with the appearance of new species and an increase in the total number of species.

Sea level always changes. The current slight sea level rise may be because of warming after the last glaciation and especially after the Little Ice Age that ended 300 years ago. The rate and amount of sea level rise is nothing extraordinary. The land level also rises and falls. There can be no discussion of sea level without a discussion of land level changes. Sea level rise can be due to the melting of ice sheets during warming but can also be due to water expansion due to ocean heating from above and below, land subsidence, displacement and heating of water due to emplacement of huge volumes of volcanic rocks on the ocean floor, gravitational pulling of mountain ranges and tectonics. Sea level has been higher than at present for most of time. Sea level fell when polar ice sheets grew, when water contracted due to cooling, when the shape of ocean basins changed and during tectonism.

Almost every catastrophic scenario painted by climate activists is a misconception and demonstrably incorrect. To ignore the history of the Earth's climate and claim that climate change is now due to human activity is extraordinary. Extraordinary conclusions require extraordinary evidence. This evidence has not been forthcoming. Science is married to evidence obtained from dispassionate repeatable measurement, experiment and observation. Methods of data collection, orders of accuracy, potential errors, replication, observational bias, assumptions, equipment limitations, standards and blanks used and data analysis methods are hotly debated before conclusions are constructed from evidence.

All data collected must be in accord with previous validated data including that from other fields of science and history. This is the scientific method. Feelings about the impending destruction of the planet as a result of increased carbon dioxide emissions are not evidence as feelings cannot be independently replicated. Scientific conclusions, albeit tentative, are based on evidence. With more evidence, re-calculation and re-evaluation of old validated evidence, the conclusions may change and hence science is never settled. Science is built on the shoulders of giants.

The scientific method has taken 2,500 years to evolve and had backward and forward steps such as in the Inquisition and Industrial Revolution respectively. Science is tribal, uses a pal review process for publication, research grants, promotion and appointments thereby maintaining the dominant elite status quo. Tribal self-interest promotes settled science and, if climate science was settled, there would be no need for further funding. Scientists are just like other people and operate from self-interest. Science advances by refutation and with funerals of scientific tribal leaders.

Climate models, on which dire warnings about the future of the planet are based, are a flawed naive attempt to simplify and try to understand evidence. Construction of models of complex non-linear chaotic multicomponent natural systems such as climate using patchy evidence are heroic because of the parameters used in model construction, the weightings of competing parameters, assumptions and unknowns. Models are not evidence and models can be tested. It appears that on the basis of models for climate in 100 years' time, we humans are going to fry and die. However, by then the modellers will be dead and not responsible for their actions.

More than 115 climate models have been constructed over the last 30 years to predict future temperature. Only one model has been in accord with past temperature measurements. This model didn't assume that atmospheric carbon dioxide drives temperature, used the Sun as the driver of climate and put a greater weighting on water vapour. All other models failed. Running models backwards has not been able to show measured temperature changes over the last 150 years or changes over the last 2,000 years when proxies give an accurate history of temperature such as the Roman and Medieval Warmings and the Dark Ages and Little Ice Age.

The concept of human-induced climate change is based on models projected well into the future and not measurement. These climate models have been tested and found wanting and restructuring of global energy systems based on fallacious climate models can only lead to economic and social trauma. For example, in late 2020 Australia's CSIRO and Bureau of Meteorology released an apocalyptic report on modelled temperature projections 100 years into the future. Such models are based on flawed data such as adjusted past and present temperatures and faulty climate-driving mechanisms such as the assumption that carbon dioxide drives atmospheric temperature. The report totally ignored the failure of previous models and ignored past and present natural climate cycles. Computer models are one of the greatest threats to mankind. We have seen this with climate change and now with COVID-19 models.

As soon as the word emissions is used, then the journey into a new dark age commences. It has never been shown that human emissions of carbon dioxide drive global warming. Human emissions are 3 per cent of total annual emissions and if it could be shown that human emissions drive global warming, it would also have to be shown that the natural emissions (97 per cent of total) do not drive global warming. Measurements of ancient air captured during snow falls and now entrapped in polar ice show that orbital-driven warming is followed nearly 1,000 years later by an increase in atmospheric carbon dioxide. Cyclical glaciations and interglacials show that atmospheric temperature controls the atmospheric carbon dioxide content and not the inverse, contrary to popular hysteria.

The first thing that a school child should learn about carbon dioxide is that it is the gas of life. Without carbon dioxide there would be no photosynthesis, no plant life and accordingly no animal life. Every time in the past when there has been warmth and/or a high atmospheric carbon dioxide content, there has been increased biodiversity and a thriving of life. In cold times, life struggles and biodiversity decreases. However, school children are taught that the gas of life is a pollutant and that human emissions must be reduced. They are also taught by radicalised teachers espousing a deep green ideology, contrary to evidence, that carbon dioxide drives global warming. The language used shows that the ideology is not underpinned by basic science. For example, carbon is black and if there were carbon emissions and carbon pollution, the skies would be black. There is no such thing as carbon pollution.

Australia produces 1.3 per cent of annual global emissions of carbon dioxide and whatever Australia does will have no effect on the global atmospheric composition because of the volume and increasing rate of emissions from the developing world, especially China and India. The slight increase in atmospheric carbon dioxide over the last half century has led to a greening of the planet, increased crop yields and, despite population increase, a decrease in deforestation and farmland. Vegetation in Australia, especially grasslands, sequester more carbon dioxide than Australians emit and the extensive continental shelf sequesters even more.

Contrary to the prevailing politically correct group think, Australia is not a net emitter of carbon dioxide and actually sequesters carbon dioxide emitted by other nations. Whatever Australia does regarding emissions, it has no effect on global climate but could have a catastrophic effect on the Australian economy.

There has been half a century of dumbing down of the education system. A school child 50 years ago probably knew far more than one today. School children are now not able to commit large bodies of information to memory, the skills of critical and analytical thinking are all but lost, reading and reflective contemplation of what has been read are not on the menu, information is gained instantly from search engines such as Google and this information is uncritically accepted. The result is that the comparative numeracy and literacy of Australian school pupils has declined alarmingly. School children are not aware that search engines are not the source of knowledge, that there are many errors and that search engines are used to promote a monocular view of certain subjects.

Instead, school pupils are indoctrinated by simplistic videos such as Al Gore's *An Inconvenient Truth*, a video that a UK Court ruled had basic scientific errors and was misleading and deceptive. These same indoctrinated pupils are persuaded to take strike action by activist climate groups such as the School Strike 4 Climate rather than attending school to learn the basics of science, history, language, rationality and logic.

This is especially the case with climate change where politicised science is promoted and those with a contrary view are denigrated. School children enter university with absolute certainty that human emissions of carbon dioxide drive global warming yet many do not know the basics such as the atmospheric content of carbon dioxide, the molecular weight of carbon dioxide, the planetary history of carbon dioxide and the simple chemistry of this gas interacting with seawater. Few university entrants have a basic knowledge of science, even fewer are able to integrate knowledge from different fields, almost none know any history or geology and one can count on a sawmiller's hand those in positions of authority that have any knowledge of basic science. The scientific method is not taught and there is no healthy scepticism or humility about scientific propositions and unknowns. A basic question such as 'How do we know what we know?' is considered a seditious and offensive question.

The story of the integrated evolution of the Earth's rocks, life, oceans and climate is an evocative natural history of the planet. The story of the planet has been determined from thousands of years of observations, measurements, experiments and calculations and integrates astronomy, geology, biology, chemistry, physics, glaciology and mathematics. The story is refined when new discoveries are made.

How many school children know that the Earth is a warm wet greenhouse volcanic planet that has had polar ice for less than 20 per cent of time? How many know that it is the Sun that drives the surface temperature of the Earth and not minuscule emissions of a trace gas by humans? How many know that reefs have been appearing and disappearing for thousands of millions of years, that reefs like any other biological system are under constant attack by predators and that changes to reefs are normal? How many know that the Earth's climate is cyclical and constantly changes? How many know that sea level can rise and fall by up to 1.5km and that at present we are living in a cool time with a relatively low sea level? How many know that the Earth's surface has been cooling for the last 5,000 years as we approach the next inevitable orbitally-driven glaciation? Do school children consider that just because there is change in our lifetime does not mean that we are the cause of this change?

It has been so easy to capture the school syllabus and teach that humans change climate when so little is known about the past. It has been so easy when history is painted as a telephone book of dates when wrongs were committed rather than a narrative of human achievements and struggles, especially with natural disasters and global coolings. Once school children have been indoctrinated and have no historical knowledge or tools of critical analysis, then the deconstruction of society can occur. Industry that emits carbon dioxide is attacked and there is a disconnect between the need for industry to maintain modern life, that carbon dioxide is plant food, that water vapour is the main greenhouse gas and that our health, communication, wealth, information and travel are all products of the Industrial Revolution.

Scientists are as frail as others and have their leaders, followers, fools, fundamentalists, fanatics and frauds. Because science is government funded, there is a tendency to follow the party line. Many professional societies survive on government grants and they too follow the popular political paradigm of the day for survival. This state control of the direction of science has resulted in a struggle between individual liberty, thought and freedoms and state control of what is considered scientifically valid. Science is conducted by teams of elites who all agree with each other in collegial consensus and those of independent thought working alone have difficulty in publishing science, winning research grants or being promoted.

Yet it is invariably these individuals who make the great discoveries because they are unconstrained, ask uncomfortable questions and question what 'everyone knows'. A good example of this is the recent discovery of the relationship between Helicobacter pylori and stomach ulcers.

Most argument about climate change in public by those who have little scientific knowledge or experience is by vulgar vicious abuse and denigration. Free speech only occurs with those who are in agreement. Every slight change or event such as bushfires is viewed without recourse to the past and, of course, we Westerners must be to blame. Communication is by social media and the thought of critically analysing all arguments is alien resulting in politically correct group think and the closing of the mind. Feelings are now the truth compared to validated scientific conclusions based on the cumulative scientific work of hundreds of scientists over decades.

Natural earth systems are dynamic, multicomponent, non-linear, chaotic and difficult to predict. To argue that traces of a trace atmospheric gas emitted by humans can drive a major planetary system is the epitome of the cancel culture mentality. Reductionist thinking into a black and white scenario with only one parameter is not science. It is politics pretending to be underpinned by science and, with the decline of Christianity in the Western world, the climate change world view has become the new fundamentalist religion of the cancel culture community.

Its holy book is the Intergovernmental Panel on Climate Change (IPCC) reports which, like other holy books, few have read. Indulgences with expensive, unreliable wind and solar electricity are purchased, the naïve and gullible seek salvation by creating saints such as the Swedish teenager Greta Thunberg, and they venerate wind and solar energy. As a result, the economic burden borne by those less wealthy is not considered and virtue signalling with expensive inefficient electric vehicles is equivalent to wearing a crucifix. Opportunistic spruikers and rent seekers can see trillions to be made by accepting government subsidies and grants and totally resetting the Western world's economy which has been based on energy from cheap plentiful fossil fuels.

The climate change cult is part of the cancel culture community masquerading as science but in reality attacks science, knowledge, education, Christianity, freedom, democracy, Western values and capitalism.

Ian Plimer is Emeritus Professor at The University of Melbourne where he was Professor and Head of Earth Sciences (1991–2005). He was also Professor of Geology at University of Newcastle (1985–1990), Ludwig Maximilans Universität, Munich (1991) and the University of Adelaide (2005–2012). He worked for North Broken Hill Ltd and is currently a director of Hancock Prospecting companies. He was on the staff of Macquarie University, The University of NSW and The University of New England, sat on numerous CSIRO and government committees and is Patron of Lifeline (Broken Hill). A Broken Hill mineral (plimerite, $ZnFe_4[PO_4]_3[OH]_5$) has been named after him for his work on the Broken Hill orebody and a northern NSW spider (Austrotengella plimeri) has been named after him for his work on climate change.

He was awarded the Leopold von Buch Medal, Centenary Medal, Eureka Prize (twice), Michael Daley Prize, Sir Willis Connolly Medal and Royal Society of NSW Clarke Medal. He is a Fellow of the Academy of Technological Sciences and Engineering, Fellow of the Geological Society of London and sat on the Australian, Swedish and German Research Councils. Professor Plimer has published more than 130 scientific papers and is author of best-selling books for the general public, the best known of which are Telling lies for God *(Random House),* Milos – geologic history *(Koan),* A short history of planet Earth *(ABC Books),* Heaven and Earth *(Connor Court) and* How to get expelled from school *(Connor Court).*

CANCEL CULTURE AND THE LEFT'S LONG MARCH: THE WAY FORWARD

STEPHEN CHAVURA

Cancel culture

Cancel culture has itself evolved out of cultural changes that have been taking place for decades, not merely in universities but in society at large. The moral revolution of the 1960s and 1970s has left many Western societies quite divided over questions of sexuality and gender, not to mention questions of culture, religion, and race relations, if not race itself. So deep and wide have the differences become that people who share the same citizenship but not the same morals often see one another as at best aliens, at worst enemies.

We can see the origins of cancel culture in the doctrines of the New Left or Neo-Marxists of the 1960s and 1970s, particularly with the idea that speech itself can be dangerous to social progress. Maybe the most influential figure of the 1960s and 1970s New Left was Herbert Marcuse, whose influential essay 'Repressive Tolerance' published in 1968 offered the following reflection on freedom of expression:

> ... tolerance cannot be indiscriminate and equal with respect to the contents of expression, neither in word nor in deed; it cannot protect false words and wrong deeds which demonstrate that they contradict and counteract the possibilities of liberation... [C]ertain things cannot be said, certain ideas

cannot be expressed, certain policies cannot be proposed, certain behavior cannot be permitted without making tolerance an instrument for the continuation of servitude.

In other words, the only speech that may be tolerated is that which conforms to a leftist social agenda. The idea that speech can harm became very popular with multicultural and critical race theorists in the 1980s and 1990s. As visions of social justice increasingly focused on race relations and multiculturalism rather than economic redistribution, more attention was focused on speech. Speech became especially interesting to critical race and gender theorists, as well as multiculturalists, because it is largely via speech that we form opinions of whole groups of people.

Typical sentiments were expressed by Mari Matsuda in her influential Michigan Law Review article 'Public Response to Racist Speech: Considering the Victim's Story'. Matsuda said, 'In addition to physical violence, there is the violence of the word'. As far back as 1989 critical race theorists were drawing an analogy between words and violence. And if the state's job is to stop and punish people who use violence on others, then rights to freedom of so-called violent speech need to be narrowed. This logic to a large extent justifies limits on free speech on some university campuses, social media platforms like Twitter and Facebook, and increasingly in corporations with activist CEOs and HR departments, not to mention public laws applying to all citizens.

The problem is that concepts such as racism, homophobia—a problematic term in itself—and misogyny have become so all-embracing that speech that is quintessentially valuable in a democracy—speech criticising immigration, same-sex marriage legislation, or feminism—is deemed hateful, harmful, and violent, and thus open to disruption, regulation, and censorship. Even in Australia during the 2017 same-sex marriage postal survey debate the leader of the opposition Labor Party, Bill Shorten, said that there should be no postal survey on the subject and no public debate because it would be detrimental to the mental health of LGBTIQ+ kids. Imagine that, no public consultation and no public debate on an issue of public law in a democracy.

The social division fuelling much of the appetite to stifle free speech and cancel those whose speech is deemed politically incorrect is most obviously the case in America. Over the past thirty years surveys have shown that increasingly progressives and conservatives find it difficult to see each other as pursuing their political and moral programmes in good faith, regardless of differences. Having said that, as Rob Henderson, a PhD candidate at the University of Cambridge, wrote in *Quillette* (2 July 2020), America's cancel culture and political correctness are being exported all around the world. Ironically, the so-called liberal democratic world, to be specific.

Cancel culture has escaped the universities and seeped into culture in general in America. Most recently the Cato Institute in 2020 carried out a survey showing that:

- 62% of Americans think the current political climate prevents them from sharing their political views,
- 50% of 'strong liberals' support firing Trump donors from their jobs, and
- 77% of conservatives feel they have to self-censor, as opposed to 52% of centrist liberals.

Note that the use of 'liberal' in this survey reflects the American meaning of that term, which is roughly synonymous with progressive or left-leaning ideology (in some ways the opposite of its meaning in Australia, and different from its meaning in the UK).

Notwithstanding the long-term causes of cancel culture, central to its most recent iteration is the prevalence of social media. John Stuart Mill famously said in his *On Liberty* (1859) that society is a much greater threat to liberty than the state, for the state is a clumsy instrument that, in the mid-nineteenth century at least, couldn't watch and control us all the time. And yet, said Mill, society— our friends, work colleagues, fellow worshippers, family, casual acquaintances—can exercise immense influence on what we dare say and how we dare live our lives. Says Mill in the Introduction to that great work, '[Society] leaves fewer means of escape, penetrating much more deeply into the details of life, and enslaving the soul itself. Protection, therefore, against the tyranny of the magistrate [government] is not enough: there needs to be protection also against the tyranny of the prevailing opinion and feeling...'

To be fair, Mill did talk about state coercion, and in all honesty the 20th century has taught us all a hard lesson on exactly what states are capable of, especially when armed with surveillance technology that is the stuff of dystopian science fiction novels like George Orwell's *1984* where Big Brother rules and citizens are under constant surveillance by the thought police. And yet social media over the last ten years lends immense credibility to Mill's claim that we ought to pay a lot of attention to how non-state forces can be decisive threats to our personal freedom to speak and live as we see fit (assuming we are not directly harming others).

In other words, for the most part, cancel culture is just what it claims to be, cultural. It is not exactly like, say McCarthyism, which was a deep conservative state hunting down Americans who expressed the wrong thoughts about communism v capitalism. That was indeed a form of cancellation, and one aided by society, but it was largely started and executed by the state. To the degree that someone would condemn the illiberal tendencies of the American state in the 1950s because of its programme of cancelling communist sympathisers, they must also condemn popular culture for allowing unfettered cancellation of citizens for expressing politically incorrect views publicly.

Widespread cancel culture in the liberal democratic West is largely a result of social media. Certainly you had instances of attempted cancellation before cancel culture. For example, in England in 1974 the sociology lectures of Caroline Cox—now Baroness Cox—at the Polytechnic of North London were routinely interrupted by Marxist protesters because she was an open Christian and critical of Marxism. Later that year university students passed a vote of no-confidence in her. Cox resigned from the university a few years later.

In Australia there was the Geoffrey Blainey Affair at Melbourne University. Professor Blainey was one of Australia's most celebrated historians when in 1984 he expressed views criticising the rate of Asian immigration to Australia and the policy of multiculturalism. His colleagues in the history department published a repudiation of his 'racialist' views and the disruptions to his classes by protesting students was so great that his classes were cancelled for the remainder of the year. His speaking engagements were also disrupted by noisy protesters.

In 1988 Blainey resigned his academic post and never held another one. These are just two well-known cases. Speak to academics or aspiring academics of a conservative nature in Britain, Australia and America and you will find that cancel culture today is just critical theory leftists doing what the traditional leftists did to conservatives for at least a generation up till now.

No medium in history has had the power to conjure up virtual mobs like social media. Within hours the reputations of individuals and the organisations they work for can be destroyed by a single Tweet, Facebook post, or YouTube video. The rapidity with which social media can make somebody famous or infamous is historically unprecedented. Naturally, in a time of deep division, that means people are very careful about what they say and do, lest their words or image be plastered all over the internet. In other words, people are self-censoring out of fear.

If there is a solution to cancel culture it is to foster a culture of debate and reasonableness, but also to praise courage in those like CEOs and university Vice-Chancellors who are in a position to resist the bullying of the cancel mob.

Cause for optimism?

Chairs and board members of corporations, Heads of Department, Deans, and Vice-Chancellors/Presidents of Universities and colleges, and anyone with the power to determine the professional fortunes of anyone who falls foul of cancel culture need to stand up to the bullies and assert the appropriateness of a diversity of opinions on contested issues. In fact, this is starting to happen around the world and it's really the major way forward in the short term.

In this respect the future of intellectual diversity isn't black, even if it is not entirely bright. For there are shining examples of academics, intellectuals, authors, CEOs, and athletes standing up for freedom of speech against cancel culture's intimidation.

In April 2018 Australian footballer Israel Folau publicly expressed his conservative Christian views on homosexuality. Immediately he faced a barrage of attacks from the twitterati, was accused by media pundits of causing LGBTIQ+ kids to commit suicide, and shortly after had his contract with Rugby Australia cancelled by the then-CEO Raelene Castle. Folau had the courage of his convictions and refused to back down and launched legal proceedings against Rugby Australia for unfair dismissal. Eventually there was an out of court settlement reportedly in the millions of dollars and Rugby Australia published an apology to Folau for his dismissal. Not long after this Castle stepped down as CEO.

In December 2019, J. K. Rowling, author of the wildly successful Harry Potter books was attacked by her Millennial fans because she defended a British researcher who lost her job for saying that 'men cannot change into women'. Rowling refused to accept the idea that male and female were not biologically determined but depended on one's sense of personal identity. 'Dress however you please. Call yourself whatever you like. Sleep with any consenting adult who'll have you. Live your best life in peace and security. But force women out of their jobs for stating that sex is real?'—tweeted the politically left-leaning Rowling. Immediately she was attacked by fans, champion mothers of trans-identifying children, and even by the young actors who played roles in the Harry Potter films. Nonetheless, Rowling stood her ground, refused to retract her words, and even signed the Harper's open letter (see below).

In August 2020, the Philadelphia Statement defending civil discourse and the strengthening of liberal democracy was released. It was signed by some of America's top academics and public intellectuals and has received over 10,000 signatures from other academics and intellectuals. The statement condemns 'blacklisting' people with unpopular (conservative) ideas, and the strategy of delegitimising reasonable conservative views on race and sexuality by deriding them as 'hateful'.

On 7 July 2020 there was an open letter published in *Harper's Magazine* signed by over 100 of America's top academics, journalists, and public intellectuals lamenting that 'it is now all too common to hear calls for swift and severe retribution in response to perceived transgressions of speech and thought. More troubling still, institutional leaders, in a spirit of panicked damage control, are delivering hasty and disproportionate punishments instead of considered reforms'. The open letter goes on to talk about capitulation to cancel culture in educational institutions as well as academic journals.

The Philadelphia Statement and the Harper's open letter are notable because they are the right and the left respectively coming together to agree on the importance of true diversity—intellectual diversity—and condemning penalties for those who fall foul of received orthodoxies.

In July 2020 Goya Foods CEO Bob Unanue visited Trump's White House to participate in an event whose topic was ways of improving Hispanic-American prosperity. As soon as the news of his participation got out Democrat Congresswoman Alexandra Ocasio-Cortez tweeted an encouragement for the company to be boycotted, as did others including Democrat politician Julian Castro, who tweeted 'Americans should think twice before buying their products'. Unanue stood his ground against the cancel mob and openly refused to apologise and retract his praise for Trump. There is an interesting lesson to be learned in this case-study, for the cancel mob assumed that Latino-Americans would agree with their view that Trump was anti-Latino. A CNN poll from the 2020 presidential election indicated that in Florida almost half of Latinos voted for Trump, up from 35 per cent in 2016. In other words, the cancellers don't necessarily represent the people they claim to be speaking for.

The Heterodox Academy began in America in 2015 and now has branches all around the world. It began as a response to the campus free speech controversies at Yale University and the University of Missouri. Heterodox Academy encourages viewpoint diversity on campuses and its own membership, unlike humanities departments in universities and colleges, has a healthy mix of conservatives and progressives, just like the actual populations of America, the UK, and Australia. Despite accusations from its detractors that the Heterodox Academy just functions to promote conservative views on campus—and we must remember that to those informed by (cultural) Marxist analysis, any opinion, no matter left or right, that is not revolutionary is reactionary—the Heterodox Academy remains staunchly committed to free speech and is a regular critic of cancel culture and politically correct uniformity on campuses.

Australia also has several think-tanks and activist organisations opposing political correctness and cancel culture including: Advance Australia, the Institute of Public Affairs, the Centre for Independent Studies, the Mannkall Economic Education Foundation and Liberty Australia.

Free speech codes

One strategy to address politically correct language and group think is for educational institutions and universities to adopt codes of free speech that encourage students to embrace open and free debate.

Across America many campuses have robust freedom of speech codes guaranteeing the right of staff and students to express ideas regardless of offence caused. The Chicago (University) 'Statement on freedom of expression' developed in 2014 affirms that the university 'guarantees all members of the University community the broadest possible latitude to speak, write, listen, challenge, and learn'. It goes on to emphasise that 'it is not the proper role of the University to attempt to shield individuals from ideas and opinions they find unwelcome, disagreeable, or even deeply offensive'. This statement has been adopted by over 60 universities and colleges in the US.

In Australia, the government released the 'Report of the Independent Review of Freedom of Speech in Australian Higher Education Providers' March 2019. Although the review actually rejected the notion that there is a 'free speech crisis' in Australian universities, it did offer a draft model code for freedom of speech to be adopted on Australian campuses 'To ensure that the freedom of lawful speech of staff and students of the university and visitors to the university is treated as a paramount value and therefore is not restricted nor its exercise unnecessarily burdened by restrictions or burdens other than those imposed by law…' Crucially, the code also affirmed that it 'does not extend to a duty to protect any person from feeling offended or shocked or insulted by the lawful speech of another'. The Review and its draft code are not perfect, but they are heading in the right direction.

Happily, all Australian universities agreed to implement the code by 2021. Of course, implementing the code does nothing to address the issue of the lack of viewpoint diversity in many university departments, particularly the humanities. As long as university departments are ideologically merely various shades of leftism, students will miss out on deep encounters with the full range of reasonable views on topics, and many students will feel pressure to ideologically conform. In other words, the French Review will do little to address the subtler forms of speech repression in universities that stem from a deficit in ideological diversity.

As well as adopting freedom of expression codes and codes prohibiting the cancellation and harassment of conservative groups on campuses, universities must also ensure that such groups are not discriminated against by student unions and woketivist administrators regarding funding, access to spaces to hold events, and unreasonable costs imposed for security against disruptive and threatening protests. The best way to make students feel safe on university campuses is not served by segregating them into narcissistic and neurotic safe-spaces, which merely encourage the delusion that they are unsafe elsewhere on campus. The better way is to expose them to ideas and debate from various perspectives that are quite common in the real off-campus world, even if they are anathema in faculty corridors. In this way they'll learn that hearing ideas with which they disagree won't really hurt them. They may even make them stronger.

Schools as nurseries of civil dialogue

It is hard to argue that a love of freedom of speech is as robust among people in liberal democracies as conservative liberals would like. During the Australian Folau case an Essential poll carried out in

July 2019 showed that 58 per cent of Australians believed employers should not have the right to dictate what their employees say outside work, while just 34 per cent believed he had the right to voice his religious views, regardless of the hurt it could cause others. In the same survey we see that 64 per cent believe that today people are unlikely to say what they really think because they are afraid of how others would react (SBS News 10/7/2019). Sadly, this clearly shows that Australians are ambivalent about robust freedom of speech as a civic right. They may not differ too much to the stats offered by the Cato Institute in America.

Having said that, Australians have also overwhelmingly stated they believe political correctness has gone too far, with the ABC in November 2019 reporting 68 per cent of Australians believing this. A more recent survey carried out in 2020 by Mark McCrindle and Mainstream Insights provides a similar figure with 65 per cent of those surveyed expressing concern about the negative impact of cancel culture and political correctness. With those under 25 the figure rose to 77 per cent expressing concern and 79 per cent stating such was the dominance of cancel culture they 'struggled to be their authentic self'.

However, looking at the ABC survey closely shows many Australians are still ambivalent about free speech. For example, the ABC reported that a clear majority of Australians—67 per cent—agreed that 'Freedom of speech is often used to justify discrimination against minority groups'. But the same proportion also agreed that 'Accusations of discrimination against minority groups are often used to try to silence legitimate debate'.

When asked 'Should people be able to say what they want, even if offends others?' the nation was divided. Forty-five per cent said yes, 45 per cent said no, with the other 10 per cent agnostic. And so the challenge is to show Australians how their instinctive antipathy towards tyrannical political correctness is best complemented by a robust commitment to freedom of speech. Unfortunately, Australians have never been known for being particularly concerned with theoretical depth.

There needs to be a strong push from state and federal education departments for school children to get used to hearing a diversity of views from platforms in the hallowed zones of their classrooms and school halls, not just in the school playground. A good way to do this is to foster a culture of debate in literature, history, and social science classes. A culture that recognises that healthy democracies thrive when citizens can distinguish between a point of view that they consider correct and a point of view that they consider reasonable. To say that a view is a reasonable one to hold is not to say that you agree with it, simply that you can understand why a reasonable person would hold it. And to say that a view is wrong is not the same as saying that it is unreasonable. Another good idea is to teach what used to be known as clear thinking at years 11 and 12.

A good model of practicing the virtues of good government is Constitution Education Fund Australia (CEFA at http://www.cefa.org.au). For around twenty years CEFA has been going into schools around Australia and running mock parliaments in which national issues are debated and voted upon, with students learning protocols of debate and decision-making procedure, as well as learning to listen to other people's points of view and offering a considered response. In other words, students are practicing the virtues that make parliamentary democracy work.

But such debates need to take differing opinions seriously. Students need to be encouraged to present two opposing sides of an issue as strongly as possible. In this way a new generation of citizens will become used to hearing articulate defences of multiple viewpoints from people of good character. But let's be honest, such a programme could fall foul of teachers, principals, school administrators, counsellors, and vocal members of the teachers unions who have been influenced by critical theory and therapeutic claims that such debates could be detrimental to children's mental health. It's an uphill battle. Most likely is that such programmes will flourish in private and independent schools whose students, parents, teachers, and principals are more likely to be open to conservative viewpoints.

Culture of bravery

At the end of the day cancel culture thrives on timidity. Even though people in general are not as passionate about free speech as we might hope, the claims of cancel culture regarding others' rights to speak freely and not have their livelihood and reputations destroyed by virtual mobs are almost certainly not as widely shared in society as they would like to think. This means that anyone who stands up for the victims of cancel culture most definitely has supporters who perhaps need some encouragement from a bold, outspoken individual to take a stand. CEOs especially need to remember that their client base is almost certainly not largely comprised of cancel culture woketivists, but that their customer base, if it reflects societies in general, will be made up of a genuine diversity of people.

The case of the company Gillette is instructive. In 2019 Gillette produced some commercials advertising their men's shaving products that criticised 'toxic masculinity', the commercials most certainly tickled the ears of woke folk, but many of the men and women found the commercials simply anti-male and preachy. In fact, there were calls to boycott Gillette—a form of cancel culture from conservatives. Months later there was a reported sharp decrease in Gillette's revenue. I am in no way endorsing calls to boycott Gillette, the point is simply to indicate that cancel culture and the woketivists don't speak for everyone, and leaders of corporations need to remember that just because cancel-criers may have the loudest voices they are not necessarily the only ones out there paying attention to what's happening.

Leaders must get educated to get confident

To be fair, we can safely assume that there are many leaders of organisations and even educational institutions out there who would like to take a stand against cancel culture but lack the intellectual weapons to do so. After all, cancel culture bases itself upon impressive sounding terms like 'systemic racism' and backs up its demands with claims that certain words and ideas are detrimental to people's mental health. Such accusations are not always easy to counter, and often the easiest thing to do is simply to capitulate rather than risk a clumsy and ill-fated opposition.

Leaders who genuinely wish to use their positions of influence to resist the pernicious influence of cancel culture in their own organisations or defend their organisations from the onslaught of cancel culture, would do well to arm themselves with the best refutations of the woke/critical theory/cultural Marxist ideology. This will not necessarily make them an expert in the areas, but it will certainly give them an articulate voice in the workplace which will make cancel culture bullies realise that they may have a fight on their hands.

A reading list would include books, articles, and podcasts on issues ranging from gender, sexuality, and race by popular and scholarly intellectuals such as Jonathan Haidt, Ben Shapiro, Brett Weinstein, Wilfred C. Reilly, Glenn Loury, Coleman Hughes, Ryan T. Anderson, Warren Farrell, the late Roger Scruton and Jordan Peterson, among others. The online Australian magazines *Quillette* and *Quadrant*, as well as the London based *The Conservative Woman* also regularly publish high-quality articles criticising many of the premises of cancel culture and political correctness. Former deputy prime minister of Australia John Anderson has brilliant and accessible interviews that are invaluable for understanding the nature of the culture wars (johnanderson.net.au).

Opponents of cancel culture must learn how to understand the use of terms such as systemic racism (Loury, Hughes, Reilly), gender pay gap (Farrell, Peterson), misogyny, and safe/unsafe (Peterson, Haidt) by cancel culture activists, and they must be able to respond to them, thus justifying their refusal to self-censor or censor and punish others who so refuse, or who have fallen foul of the woketivists ideology.

Conclusion

There is no silver bullet for cancel culture and the neo-Marxist-postmodernist-inspired campaign to enforce language control and group think. It takes above all courage. It would be nice to think that citizens will over time learn to see the pernicious nature of cancel culture and develop a re-appreciation for the boon of freedom of speech for society. Alas, we cannot count on this. At least just as likely is that cancel culture will evanesce as increasingly people make self-censorship unconscious habit. In other words, cancel culture triumphs quietly.

As so many theologians, philosophers, and social theorists warned us throughout the twentieth century, with luxury, technology, ease, and entertainment comes civic apathy and indifference to anything that does not award one with an immediate dopamine hit. This is why codes of free speech and programmes exposing children to genuine diversity of ideas in schools are so important. Sadly, it may be the case that in a prosperous and relatively peaceful society people's natural inclination is to prefer to either not think or be told what to think rather than to think for themselves. Having said that, the last five years—Brexit, Trump's 2016 election, the 2020 US election—have also shown that there are large portions of populations who strongly resist leftist groupthink. Whether these flourishes of ideological contrarianism are the swan song or Phoenix of free-thinking civic activism is yet to be seen.

Dr. Stephen Chavura, Ph.D., teaches European and Australian history at Campion College, Sydney. Before he worked at Campion he was a lecturer in sociology and political philosophy at various Australian universities. He has published in numerous journals including History of European Ideas, Journal of Religious History, *and* Australian Journal of Political Science. *His most recent (co-authored) books are* The Forgotten Menzies: The Mind of Australia's Longest-Serving Prime Minister *(2021), and* Reason, Religion, and the Australian Polity: A Secular State? *(2019). He also writes opinion pieces on current affairs that have appeared in* The Australian, Spectator Australia, *and* ABC Religion and Ethics.